ARNOLD WESKER

The Merchant

With Commentary and Notes by
GLENDA LEEMING

Methuen Student Editions
METHUEN · LONDON

This Methuen Student Edition first published in 1983 by
Methuen London Ltd., 11 New Fetter Lane, London EC4P 4EE.

The Merchant first published in East Germany by Henschel
Verlag 1977. Revised edition published in Penguin Books 1980.
Further revised for this edition 1983.
Copyright © Arnold Wesker 1977, 1983.
Author's preface © Arnold Wesker 1981.
Commentary and Notes copyright © 1983 by Methuen London Ltd.

ISBN 0 413 51620 2

Set in IBM 10 point Journal by 𝓕\ Tek-Art, Croydon, Surrey
Printed in Great Britain by
Richard Clay (The Chaucer Press) Ltd,
Bungay, Suffolk

*Thanks are due to Arnold Wesker for his help and advice — and
loan of photographs — during the preparation of this edition.*

Contents

Arnold Wesker: a chronology

1932 Born in East End of London: father, Joseph Wesker, a
Russian-Jewish tailor; mother, Leah Wesker,
Hungarian-Jewish.

1939 Evacuated briefly to various parts of England and Wales, but
spent most of the war period at home. Lived with parents
when in London until his marriage.

1943 Failed eleven plus, and went to Upton House Central School,
which emphasised clerical studies. Enjoyed amateur acting
outside school.

1948 Left school and worked at many jobs, including carpenter's
mate, bookseller's assistant and plumber's mate.

1950 Two years National Service in the Royal Air Force. Formed
-52 drama group for enlisted airmen. Wrote a series of diary-style
letters which were later shaped into an novel (unpublished)
and finally used as the raw material for *Chips With Everything*.

1952 Several jobs in London and Norfolk — plumber's mate, seed
-56 sorter, farm labourer, kitchen porter — then returned to
London, where he spent two years as a pastry cook.

1956 Worked in Paris for nine months as a chef, saving money to
enter the London School of Film Technique.

1957 Met Lindsay Anderson by chance and asked him to read his
short story *Pools*, as possible subject for a film. Although this
came to nothing, Anderson read *Chicken Soup With Barley*
and *The Kitchen* and sent them to George Devine at the
Royal Court Theatre.

1958 First production of *Chicken Soup With Barley* directed by
John Dexter at the Belgrade Theatre, Coventry. This
transferred to London to the Royal Court for a second week.
Awarded Arts Council grant of £300, which he used to marry
Doreen Bicker, whom he had met while both were working in
The Bell Hotel, Norwich.

1959 *Roots* and *The Kitchen* first produced. *Evening Standard's*
Most Promising Playwright Award for *Roots*.

1960 *Chicken Soup With Barley*, *Roots* and *I'm Talking About
Jerusalem* produced as *The Wesker Trilogy* at the Royal

Court, opening on 7 June, 28 June, and 27 July respectively.

1961 *Roots* was Wesker's first play to be produced in the USA: the off-Broadway production received mixed notices. *The Kitchen:* revised version staged at Royal Court, and film version released. Demonstrated against use of nuclear weapons along with other writers, and sentenced to one month in prison. Accepted directorship of Centre Fortytwo, a cultural movement for making the arts more widely accessible, primarily through trade union support and involvement.

1962 *Chips With Everything* opened and voted Best Play of 1962. Wesker inaugurated the idea of simultaneous productions in the provinces, with openings in Glasgow and Sheffield a few days after the London premiere. *Chips* transferred to West End.

1963 *Chips With Everything* opened on Broadway to good notices. *Menace* on BBC-TV.

1964 *Their Very Own and Golden City* won Italian Premio Marzotto drama award.

1965 Off-Broadway production of *The Kitchen* achieved a six-month run to good notices. *The Four Seasons* opened at the Belgrade, Coventry, transferred to West End.

1966 *Their Very Own and Golden City:* world premiere in Belgium, then British premiere at Royal Court.

1967 Off-Broadway production of *The Four Seasons:* badly received.

1970 After directing his own *The Friends* first in Stockholm then at the Roundhouse, Wesker resigned from the Roundhouse Trust and on 20 December persuaded the Council for Centre Fortytwo to pass a resolution dissolving itself. *Fears of Fragmentation,* a collection of lectures and articles, published.

1971 *Six Sundays in January,* a collection of stories, published.

1972 *The Old Ones* opened at Royal Court.

1973 *The Kitchen* won gold medal in Spain.

1974 *The Old Ones* well received in a workshop production off-Broadway. *The Wedding Feast:* world premiere in Stockholm. *Love Letters on Blue Paper,* a collection of stories, published.

1976 Sales of the Penguin edition of *The Wesker Trilogy* reached quarter of a million. BBC-1 TV presentation of *Love Letters on Blue Paper.* World premiere of *The Merchant* at the Stockholm Royal Dramaten, 8 October.

1977 British premiere of *The Wedding Feast*, Leeds Playhouse, 20 January. World premiere of *The Journalists* at the Criterion Theatre, Coventry (amateur production), 26 March. World premiere of *Love Letters on Blue Paper*, Syracuse (USA). English-speaking premiere of *The Merchant*, New York, 16 November.

1978 *The Merchant:* British premiere, Birmingham Repertory Theatre, 12 October. *Love Letters on Blue Paper* opened at the National Theatre's Cottesloe auditorium, directed by the author, 15 February. *Said the Old Man to the Young Man,* a collection of stories, published.

1979 *Chicken Soup* wins gold medal as best foreign play at National Theatre Madrid. Wesker commissioned to write film script of the *Trilogy*, financed by National Film Development Fund. *The Journalists — a Triptych,* published.

1980 Commissioned by the touring theatres of Norway, Sweden and Denmark to write a new play: this play, *Caritas,* completed in July. *One More Ride on the Merry-Go-Round* written under a pseudonym in 1978 now revised and pseudonym dropped. Original film script, *Lady Othello,* written, and TV play, *Whitsun,* adapted from story *The Visit. Love Letters on Blue Paper and Other Stories,* an anthology from earlier collections of stories, published.

1981 Premiere of *Caritas* at the National Theatre's Cottesloe auditorium on 7 October. Professional premiere of *The Journalists* 10 October at Wilhelmshaven, Germany. First draft of *Breakfast,* short play for television. Adaptation of *The Four Seasons* for television. First draft of one-act comedy, *Sullied Hands. Annie Wobbler,* monologues for solo voice written specially for actress Nichola McAuliffe.

1982 *Mothers,* a set of four portraits on the theme of the mother, commissioned by Koichi Kimura for Tokyo festival of one-act plays, where it was premiered 2 July, directed by Tsunetoshi Hirowatarai.

1983 *Annie Wobbler* first performed by Süddeutscher Rundfunk under title *Annie, Anna, Annabella,* 3 February. World premiere directed by author for Birmingham Rep. Studio Theatre, 30 June (press night, 5 July).

Plot

You are a Jew, Shylock. Not only is your race a minority, it is
despised. Your existence here in Venice, your pleasures, your
very freedom to be sardonic or bitter is a privilege, not a right.
Your life, the lives of your people depend upon contract and
your respect for the laws behind contract, just as your contract
with the city councillors they must respect. The law, Shylock,
the law! For you and your people, the bond-in-law must be
honoured. (p. 25)

The driving force of the plot is the anti-Jewish feeling in Venice
and in Europe generally. The action takes place in Venice in 1563.

Act I Scene 1
The first scene is set in the Ghetto Nuovo, in which the Jews of
Venice have by law to live. Antonio, a Venetian patrician and
merchant is helping the Jewish Shylock to bring out and catalogue
his books, and we quickly learn that their close friendship is an
exception to the climate of anti-Jewish feeling in Venice which,
amongst other oppressions, would have destroyed Shylock's
Hebrew books if he had not hidden them. Antonio is also an
exception. Unlike most Venetians he regrets years wasted in trade,
to the neglect of knowledge and curiosity, the attributes he values
in Shylock.

Act I Scene II
Though Shylock and Antonio here discuss the problems of the
Jews again, while drinking together after the cataloguing is
finished, the main function of this scene is to describe the
imminent arrival of Bassanio, Antonio's godson but a stranger to
him, and to establish that Antonio is too drunk and weary to leave
the Ghetto that night, so that his first meeting with Bassanio will
take place in the Ghetto.

Act I Scene III

The next morning we see a typical scene in Shylock's household, which is lively, turbulent and welcoming like his own character. His sister Rivka is equally hospitable. However, his daughter Jessica is resentful, finding his energy too demanding, and the over-extension of these energies is demonstrated when his partner Tubal and the young architect Rodriguez find it difficult to get Shylock to attend to his affairs with them. Two new visitors from Portugal, Solomon Usque and Rebecca da Mendes, bring news that provides a background to the Jews' oppression in Venice: elsewhere oppression is much worse, and they describe the burning alive of Jews in Portugal by the Inquisition — thus fear of similar persecution must be in the back of the minds even of the tolerated Venetian Jews. The behaviour of Bassanio, arriving at this point, illustrates the threat as his evident suspicion and contempt for the Jews is based not on knowledge but hearsay — he admits he has never even seen a Jew before. His request inaugurates the main thread of the plot, as he wishes to borrow a large sum of money from Antonio. He explains that he wishes to try the prescribed test of choosing the right casket to win the heiress Portia, but, having led a wasteful life, needs more money to present himself as a suitable husband. Antonio has laid out all his assets at once in a series of trading voyages and says, to Bassanio's horror, that only his friend Shylock will lend him money in his present insecure financial position. After Bassanio has gone, Shylock at once agrees to the loan which he wishes to be free of interest or security. Here Antonio raises the key point on which the rest of the plot depends — by law all dealings between Jew and gentile must be formally registered with all details specified, and any tampering with the law would leave the Jews without the security against persecution that the law gives them. Shylock's suggestion of the bond demanding a forfeit of a pound of flesh for non-payment is a joke against the law which, while protecting him, denies the right to simple human trust between the two races. Finally Antonio agrees to this joke.

Act I Scene IV

Three young men of Venice, Bassanio, his friend the discontented poet Lorenzo, and Antonio's foolish clerk Graziano, discuss their dislike of the Jews and of Shylock in particular. Lorenzo reveals that he is friendly with and attracted to Jessica. He also complains that the older patricians exclude the younger ones from power, and he himself would like the power to make the government of

Venice more moral and less tolerant. This launches them into a debate about the very nature of power, which is the theme of the play. Bassanio argues that the traditional priority Venice puts on trade has kept the state from the extremes of fanatical wars or unprofitable persecutions. Graziano merely has a confused sense that what is important is the linking of power to families which like his own already have aristocratic traditions of power.

Act I Scene V

Much of this scene, which takes place while Shylock and his family pose for their portrait by the octogenarian painter Moses of Castelazzo, is taken up with a quarrel between Shylock and Jessica, after which she storms out: this underlines the danger that, as Usque says, her father's dominance will 'drive her into a hasty marriage'.

Act I Scene VI

At dinner at Antonio's house, dissension arises between Shylock and the other guests, Bassanio, Graziano and Lorenzo, who continue their earlier debate about power and its relation to trade, tradition or moral position. Antonio supports the materialist 'trade' view, but Shylock opposes all of them, and argues that the trade and prosperity of Venice as a city-state depend on principles, knowledge and systems derived from classical learning. To prove this he traces the history of how classical texts survived the dark ages, the intrinsic value of the knowledge somehow recognised by the different groups of men who handed it on. In spite of this however Shylock is still subject to the narrow-minded rules that make him wear a yellow hat and return to the Ghetto by curfew. Yet at this point of the play his outlook seems to include more optimism than pessimism.

Act II Scene I

Portia is just entering on her inheritance of ruined estates, neglected by her unworldly philosopher father. He has also required that she marry the suitor who chooses the right casket from a choice of gold, silver and lead. Her mother was an energetic peasant woman, and Portia feels herself to be exceptional, both in her practical energy and in her strong and well-educated intellect. As Antonio values Shylock's knowledge and intellectual curiosity, so Portia wishes to ensure the education of her maid Nerissa.

Act II Scene II

Bassanio has to choose between gold, silver and lead caskets, and
does so by subtly assessing the character of his 'opponent' —
Portia's dead father. He works out that a ruined, despairing
philosopher would require a rich competent husband to save his
daughter from poverty, a man who would value gold in the first
place — but being essentially a foolish philosopher, her father
would then have changed his mind at the last minute — so the
answer is the lead casket. His success is a coolly calculated one, and
Portia, though attracted to him, is wary of his self-interested
attitude. Alone together, she and Nerissa question masculine
values, a foretaste of the independence that later carries them to
the Venetian court.

Act II Scene III

By contrast, Shylock's fortunes suddenly sink, as do Antonio's.
From the questions of Tubal and Rodriguez we hear that Jessica
has run away, and Antonio's ships, in which his money is bound
up, may be wrecked or captured and in any case cannot return
before the bond is due in two days' time. Graziano confirms the
news, then we see Jessica meet Lorenzo, ready to elope with him.

Act II Scene IV

Shylock at home can hardly attend to the dangerous bond because
he is distressed by the loss of his beloved daughter. His sister Rivka
points out that he cannot allow the law to be waived, in case this
forms a precedent for ignoring their laws protecting Jews. When
Antonio comes Shylock pretends to think that something will turn
up to save them, but Antonio insists that he face the facts. Tubal
and Rodriguez bring the bad news that it is Lorenzo with whom
Jessica has fled, and Graziano once more arrives to confirm
officially that all Antonio's ships are captured or sunk. Left alone,
Antonio and Shylock discuss their predicament. They cannot
escape the legal machinery they have set in motion themselves, and
Shylock asks that Antonio should not explain that Shylock has
good and urgent motives for not weakening the power of the law.

Act II Scene V

As soon as Jessica and Lorenzo reach Belmont, the final phase of
the plot begins. Their news of the forfeiture of the bond provokes
harsh and intolerant comments about Shylock from the young
men, which in turn antagonises Jessica. Lorenzo's attempt

thereupon to convert her from Judaism to Christianity alienates
her further and she becomes aware of the distance between them.
After the men have left to attend the Venetian court, Portia
sympathises with Jessica and, at Nerissa's suggestion, considers
going to the trial too: at this point she has the inspiration that
there is a loophole in the law.

Act II Scene VI
Portia, Nerissa and Jessica enter the Venetian courtroom where
Bassanio, Lorenzo, Graziano and other Venetian citizens have been
for two hours already, baffled by Antonio's and Shylock's silence.
The doge is trying yet again to discover why the bond was made
and why the two participants will not agree to have the law set
aside. Lorenzo argues that the blame lies with the system of
money-lending as such, and the unsatisfactory government that
permits it, rather than with the Jews as a race, but Shylock angrily
rejects his defence as patronising — his Jewishness should need no
excuse. It is Graziano's more straightforward anti-Jewish insults
however that make him demand a quick end to the arguments,
insisting on his pound of flesh. As the tension mounts Portia
intervenes and points out that the bond is impracticable, as it is
impossible to cut an exact weight of flesh without bloodshed, and
therefore the whole contract is invalid. Shylock is ecstatically
thankful — his friend is saved, without the protective laws being
undermined. However the doge cites an old Venetian law that
takes the life and property of any alien who plots against a
Venetian citizen. He grants Shylock his life, but confiscates his
goods, including his beloved books. Crushed once more by
inflexible laws, Shylock reverts to his former bitterness.

Act II Scene VII
Two weeks later at Belmont, Bassanio, Lorenzo and Graziano are
having a farewell supper and reminiscing over the trial and what
they see as Shylock's discomfiture. Jessica by now is disillusioned
with and contemptuous of Lorenzo. Portia tells Antonio that she
also is disillusioned with Bassanio, and though she will marry him
she intends to keep him under her control, and fill her life with
other interests, economic, political and cultural — but she will
make sure that Jessica does not have to marry Lorenzo. Antonio
too, who is about to see Shylock off on a pilgrimage to Jerusalem,
expects to face a less fulfilled life without his friend, but intends to
endure it with as good a grace as he can. Antonio, Portia and

Jessica have all had their high hopes of happiness diminished and are melancholy, but meanwhile the complacent young Venetians laugh, and Nerissa mockingly tells them what heroes they are.

Commentary

Historical background

It is not really certain what made the first Venetian settlers brave the inconvenience of the islands in the tide-washed lagoon: the favourite story is that these settlers were refugees from the advancing hordes of Attila the Hun, but, as Graziano says, the prosperous citizens of Venice later preferred to forget that for centuries their ancestors had been fishermen, possibly small traders. Gradually as population and trade increased, Venice developed social and political systems parallel to, but different from, the other city states of mediaeval Italy. Its combination of democracy and oligarchy fluctuated over the generations: as Graziano again says, the first doges were elected in the Dark Ages (697) and other bodies of government were at first elected by all the male inhabitants of the city, but successive alterations to the constitution curtailed this franchise, until during the period of *The Merchant* only the patricians who could prove descent from the original members of the Great Council, could vote for the Senate, which in turn voted for other officers. And even patricians could only vote if they were over the age of twenty-five, which is why Lorenzo complains throughout the play that young men are excluded from the slightest vestige of political power.

Venice became rich and powerful through trade, as Antonio and Bassanio insist, and this meant that money-lending — another kind of trading, after all — was a touchy question. One of the justifications of the 'scapegoat' persecutions of the Jews was that so many Jews practised usury, that is, simply the lending of money to be paid back with an additional sum as interest, which, theologians argued, was sinful and forbidden by the Bible (e.g. *Deuteronomy* 23, 19—20). Even Aristotle, the respectable secular authority of classical times, had specificallycondemned usury as being unnatural — making money out of money, rather than by producing goods. This is the basis of Lorenzo's 'Money is a dead thing with no seed, it's not fit to engender' (p. 27). But to some mediaeval thinkers, all retail trading was, on the same grounds, also sinful. The right way to live was by producing goods, not gaining profit by acting as middleman.

Thus the growth of trade and capital generally caused some uneasiness. W.H. Auden notes that 'A change in the nature of wealth from landownership to money capital radically alters the social conception of time' in that 'the social conception of time in a landowning society is cyclical — the future is expected to be a repetition of the past' as opposed to a free-wheeling mercantile society where 'the future is always novel and unpredictable'. Portia, for one, rejects this unpredictability to return to the cyclical and productive values of landowning. On the other hand, the unpredictability favoured lively minds like Shylock's and undermined the aristocratic traditions that repressed developments of various kinds in other city states:

> The merchant is constantly taking risks — if he is lucky, he may make a fortune, if he is unlucky he may lose everything. Since, in a mercantile society, social power is derived from money, the distribution of power within it is constantly changing, which has the effect of weakening reverence for the past; who one's distant ancestors were soon ceases to be of much social importance. The oath of lifelong loyalty is replaced by the contract, which binds its signatories to fulfil certain specific promises by a certain specific future date, after which their commitment to each other is over. (W.H. Auden, *The Dyer's Hand*, p. 220)

Mercantile Venice, then, was not untouched by the same brush that painted the Jews as money-breeders. Mary McCarthy makes a direct comparison:

> Anti-semitism is often traced to a mediaeval hatred of capitalism. To the mediaeval mind, the Jew was the capitalist *par excellence*. But this could also be said of the Venetian, whose palace was his emporium and his warehouse. (Mary McCarthy, *Venice Observed*, Heinemann, 1961, p. 36)

However, it is easy to distinguish the Jews from native European capitalists by race and religion, and the distinction found physical expression in their segregation into the Ghetto:

> The Venetians were tolerant, but the Ghetto was a Venetian invention, a typical piece of Venetian machinery, designed to 'contain' the Jews while profiting from them, just as the doge was 'contained'. The word comes from the Venetian word, foundry, and the New Ghetto, into which the Jews were

directed, the day after Pentecost, 1516, was the New Foundry, where cannons had formerly been cast . . . Venetian geography made segregation easy. The area of the New Foundry was an island, on which the Jews were shut up every day at nightfall. The three gates were closed and locked. Christian guards, paid by the Jews, were posted, at first in boats on the canal. The house windows facing outwards were blocked up, by decree, so that the Ghetto turned a blind face to the city . . . When crowding became a problem, tall houses resembling skyscrapers were built, which still can be seen in the main square of the Ghetto Nuovo — a strange, picturesque sight, as if a modern slum were expressed in an ancient idiom, like a prophecy. (*Venice Observed*, pp. 52–3)

This is why Antonio cannot leave the Ghetto after curfew, and why it is so dangerous for the inmates of the Ghetto to be out searching for Jessica after nightfall.

Wesker made the pivot of his play the bond, both in its implied lack of human 'commitment', as Auden put it, even between friends, and in its special significance for the Jews. Mary McCarthy quotes Shakespeare's lines in *The Merchant of Venice*:

The Duke cannot deny the course of law:
For the commodity that strangers have
With us in Venice, if it be denied,
Will much impeach the justice of the State,
Since that the trade and profit of the city
Consisteth of all nations. (III iii)

and comments on the ulterior motives of this admirable tolerance:

Here the Venetian cash-register rings, for if the Republic tolerated the Jews, it did so for a price. No Jew, including a native, could stay in Venice without a permit, which cost a considerable sum of money, and which had to be renewed every five, seven, or ten years for an additional fee . . . the Jews had no recourse, generally, but to pay the price set by the Republic for its continued toleration. The notion that a Jew had rights did not imply any doctrine of equality; the Jews had *specific* rights, the rights he paid to enjoy. (*Venice Observed*, p. 52)

As Tubal says, 'We survive from contract to contract . . .' (p. 15). The very existence of the laws of contract proves that the Jews were threatened — if they were not constantly at risk they would not need special legal protection, and it was an insult to them that they were not allowed to form even normal business relationships with other races. The apparent protection also gave opportunity for exploitation, as Mary McCarthy points out:

> But for all this the Venetians exacted a veritable pound of flesh. They bled the Jewish community in every conceivable way. Since the law forbade Jews to own land, the Republic forced them to *rent* the Ghetto in its entirety on a long lease; the day the Jews moved in, rentals were raised one-third. In the course of years, many Jews left Venice for Holland, because of Venetian rapacity; others died of the plague. But the community continued to pay rent on houses that stood unoccupied — that was the contract. They were gouged for taxes, for tribute, for the army, for the navy, for the upkeep of the canals; they were forced to keep open their loan banks and to pay the government for the privilege, long after these had ceased to be profitable. They were not permitted to go out of business, just as the doge was not permitted to refuse his office or to resign it. This relentless policy continued to the point where in 1735, the *Inquisitori sopra gli Ebrei* had to confess to the Senate that the Jews under their supervision were insolvent, and the community was declared bankrupt, by official state decree. There was no more to be got from them, the Venetians, as realists, conceded, crossing the account off their books with one of those resigned shrugs commonly thought of as Jewish. (*Venice Observed*, p. 55)

Again, Tubal's list of 'annual tributes' is authentic. And the rights the Jews bought by these payments were still far enough from equality that other laws aimed specifically against aliens could outweigh these lesser rights. Auden's distinction between brothers and others is at the heart of Wesker's play:

> At the last moment when, through his conduct, Shylock has destroyed any sympathy we may have felt for him earlier, we are reminded that, irrespective of this personal character, his status is one of inferiority. A Jew is not regarded, even in law, as a brother. (*The Dyer's Hand*, p. 229)

How the play came to be written

As Wesker says in his preface, the initial impulse to write his version of Shakespeare's *The Merchant of Venice* came

> when, in 1973, watching Laurence Olivier's oi-yoi-yoi portrayal of Shylock in Jonathan Miller's production at the National, I

was struck by the play's irredeemable anti-semitism. It was not
an intellectual evaluation but the immediate impact I actually
experienced.

Wesker is a writer who tends to write from his own experience,
and as a Jew himself, feeling that 'Neither in Miller's production,
nor in any other I've seen, could I recognise a Jew I knew', he set
about presenting the experience of living in a Jewish community as
he knew it, though his own experience was of course several
centuries later than Shylock's.

He was influenced by three main considerations. Firstly, the
fact that during the Second World War (1939–45) six million Jews
were killed in concentration camps by the Nazis reminds us that
persecution of the Jews over bygone centuries can recur in an even
worse form in an age which ought to have become more
enlightened. Remembering this, audiences today are at least
intermittently uneasy at seeing the Jew presented as an inhuman
villain, because they are aware that this sort of portrayal has been
used in living memory as an excuse for persecution. A second
consideration is that the state of Israel, established in 1948 as a
home for the Jewish nation, is involved in military and political
conflicts, and international opinion towards it may be influenced
by residues of the old anti-semitic prejudice. Thirdly, prejudice
against Jews is still common to a greater or lesser degree in most
societies, affecting the victims' lives adversely without necessarily
amounting to outright persecution. So, for all these reasons,
Wesker started to work on the play, 'not, it must be noted,
unaffected by the sight of the world abandoning the Jews after the
Yom Kippur War' (October 1973) and with a 'growing sense of
responsibility towards the Jewish image' (quoted from Wesker's
unpublished diary).

After his first thought that he would simply direct Shakespeare's
play with certain changes, he soon 'realised that it would be
simpler to write a new play' (*Theatre Quarterly* 28 p. 21) The
point of departure then was his sense of knowing better than
Shakespeare did how Shylock as a Jew would have felt and acted:

> The *real* Shylock would not have torn his hair out and raged
> against not being allowed to cut his pound of flesh, but would
> have said 'Thank God!' The point of writing a play in which
> Shylock would utter these words would be to explain how he
> became involved in such a bond in the first place. (Preface)

Such a change of motivation in the bond plot involved a radical alteration of the play:

> My first notes show that the characters were going to be completely reconceived and I sloughed off more and more of the original as I went along. For example, some early notes show how I was going to handle the Lancelot Gobbo scenes, but in the end I dispensed with them entirely. (*Theatre Quarterly* 28, p.22)

Finding new reasons for Shylock's bond meant research into the history of the Jews in Venice, and some groundwork was done here by the students of a summer school at the University of Colorado. Wesker began teaching a course on contemporary dramatists there in 1974, but found this was distracting him maddeningly from the new play he was trying to evolve, so he suggested to the students that instead they should help him with his play — to which they enthusiastically agreed.

> I divided the class into three parts, asked each to tackle a third of Shakespeare's play, break it down, comment on it. And then I urged them to think about my approach and see if it was justified, plausible. The class talked and delivered me essays and papers. But one, a postgraduate student, quite outstanding from the rest, went to work with an especially excited drive and presented me with three papers. One on 'Portia', another on 'The Merchant Metamorphosed', another on 'Jews in the Renaissance — Mostly Bibliography'. She used scholarship to vindicate and encourage me in my instinctive approach, she began my reading list and, most invaluable, she discovered for me a fact about Venetian society and its relationship with the Jews which became one of the pillars of the play, namely: that no Venetian could have dealings with a Jew unless a contract existed. Lois Bueler is her name. I dedicated the play to her. (Diary)

Back in Britain, he went to his cottage in the Welsh mountains and from September 1974 to February 1975 submerged himself in reading for the play — on Renaissance history, the development of printing, the position of women in the sixteenth century and so on. When it came to actually beginning to write, the creative process was a fairly painful one:

> Yesterday, after anxiously inching my way these months toward beginning *The Merchant*, I began. A day to celebrate! Was

thrilled and tense, but confident. Could feel it all in me. It would be a bold, stunning new *Merchant*. The peak of my dramatic skills! . . . Decided to go back to the beginning of what I'd written. Fatal! By the second page it seemed, in an instant, that I'd no play to write after all. This, the most 'brilliant of my works' was a flabby, wordy, historically and racially self-conscious bore. It had been a phantom pregnancy.

And here I am, in the middle of the Black Mountains, isolated and alone with this dreadful discovery, this unbearable knowledge, and not even a vehicle into which I can throw my bags and leave. And yet I feel I ought to force myself to look at the script again. To start savagely cutting and rewriting. It's as though I ought to go back and look at a dead body just in case I've panicked and it's really still breathing. If I leave it now, then by morning perhaps it'll really be dead.

My God! How did I write all those other plays! (Diary)

In fact he did savagely cut and rewrite to his own satisfaction, and by April was recording

The Merchant continues. Grows rich and succulent in arias and argument and historical colouring. But over-ripe I fear. It'll run for four hours in the first draft, I bet, and then will have to be cut'. (Diary)

In August he finished the second typed draft of the whole play, and admitted 'I'm — kind of — happy'.

This was the point at which the play was sent to theatre managements and individuals; the later changes, including cuts, took place during rehearsal.

'The Merchant' and 'The Merchant of Venice'

Shakespeare wove his play *The Merchant of Venice* from three extant sources. First, a story written in Italian at the end of the fourteenth century about a rich merchant of Venice called Angaldo who borrows money against a pound of flesh from a Jew so that his 'godson' Giannetto can seek his fortune. Second, a story about wooing and needing to choose the right casket out of three in order to secure the woman for a wife. And third, probably, a fifteenth century story by Masuccio di Salerno about a daughter escaping with her miserly father's jewels to her love aided by a slave. (Diary: Wesker summarises these sources from John Russell Brown's introduction to the Arden edition of *The Merchant of Venice*.)

Shakespeare's three basic plot lines, based on these sources, were all kept in *The Merchant,* but changed, either by altering important elements in them, or by giving the original elements a new significance. For instance, a major change was to make Shylock a sympathetic character and a friend of Antonio. And a change in significance follows from this — his daughter Jessica still runs away with a gentile, but her flight now becomes a bid for freedom from an over-possessive but loving father, not escape from a miserly old tyrant. The conflict of black and white becomes a conflict of differing psychologies.

The basic change in the play as a whole, focused by the shift in Shylock's character is the way that anti-Jewish feeling is presented. In Shakespeare's play it is taken for granted; it is the foundation and background to Shylock's character as a villain: all Jews are supposed to be miserly, so Shylock is miserly — not as his individual characteristic, as with Molière's Harpagon, but simply because he is a Jew. This view is hardly questioned, except in Shylock's famous 'hath not a Jew eyes' speech. An anti-semitic attitude, in short, is common to the non-Jewish Venetian characters, and it is their society which dominates Shakespeare's play.

But in Wesker's *The Merchant* this attitude is not left in the background — it is discussed and questioned explicitly. Proportionally more of his characters are Jewish and many scenes are devoted to their lives, showing both their pleasant unexceptional personalities and the effect on them of hostile prejudice. They are hemmed in by rules and regulations, shut into their Ghetto from evening curfew every night, with the gentiles shut out: unlike Shakespeare's Shylock, whose house apparently is on the 'public street' where 'Christian fools' are free to pass all night (II v). Moreover, there is always the knowledge of the torture and killing of Jews in other countries, such as Rebecca and Usque describe, to remind them that hostility might well become much worse. Of the Venetians, the more sympathetic characters, Antonio and Portia, are exceptional in their friendship towards the Jews, and those who express the general anti-semitism, such as Bassanio, Lorenzo and Graziano, are thoughtless and biased in their attitudes towards other issues too, such as power, religion and the position of women.

An important factor in Wesker's rewriting was the change in the audience's view of the plot. Apart from giving his personal reactions to Shylock, Wesker's objections echo those of various

other critics. Muriel Bradbrook agrees that the presentation of
Shylock by Shakespeare is hostile:

> The personal responsibility of Shylock for his horrible state is
> very small; it is the result of his wrongs, his birth, and his creed.
> But to remove all guilt from him on this account, and to treat
> him as a sympathetic criminal, would not have occurred to any
> Elizabethan. (*Shakespeare and Elizabethan Poetry*, p. 2)

And W.H. Auden, referring to the attempted extermination of the
Jewish people by the Nazis, argues that the simple Elizabethan
position is not open to a modern audience:

> Recent history has made it utterly impossible for the most
> unsophisticated and ignorant audience to ignore the historical
> reality of the Jews and think of them as fairy-story bogeys with
> huge noses and red wigs. An Elizabethan audience undoubtedly
> still could − very few of them had seen a Jew − and, if
> Shakespeare had so wished, he could have made Shylock
> grotesquely wicked like the Jew of Malta. (*The Dyer's Hand*,
> p. 223)

In rewriting the play, Wesker embodied present-day feelings about
Shylock's role, both in making him a consistent character, and in
facing up to the question of 'his wrongs, his birth and his creed.'
Many of the specific changes to character and plot follow from this
basic change of attitude. Shakespeare's Shylock proposes a 'merry
bond', but he does not *mean* this merrily, whereas Wesker's
Shylock is perfectly sincere in *not* meaning his 'nonsense bond' to
be taken seriously. Both Shylocks are finally caught up in and
crushed by the legal machinery they themselves set in motion, but
in Shakespeare's play the law fulfills its proper purpose, and in the
later play its destructiveness leads us to question its values.

Similarly, the twentieth century's changed opinions on other
issues, such as the relationship of parents and children, and the
position of women in society, give a new signficance to the original
plot elements. In Shakespeare, the proposal that Portia should have
to marry the suitor who passes her dead father's test is an arbitrary
situation, but is accepted as the sort of thing that happens in a folk
tale. In Wesker's play the same situation is still arbitrary, but is
therefore seen as *wrong*, because in the real world human
relationships ought not to be dictated by such silly tests,
symbolising all the irrelevant and unsuitable conditions that are
imposed on dependent women by their menfolk. Another opinion

that has changed concerns the right of a young gentleman to an
unearned income, possibly by marrying an heiress. Such 'marrying
for money' is looked at critically today when earned income is
respected, so Bassanio becomes a somewhat mercenary,
self-centred opportunist, instead of the conventional hero of folk
tale seeking his fortune. And Jessica's elopement likewise
is uncomfortable for a modern audience. As Auden says:

> Lorenzo and Jessica, for all their beauty and charm, appear as
> frivolous members of a leisure class, whose carefree life is
> parasitic upon the labours of others, including usurers. When we
> learn that Jessica has spent fourscore ducats of her father's
> money in an evening and bought a monkey with her mother's
> ring, we cannot take this as a comic punishment for Shylock's
> sin of avarice; her behaviour seems rather an example of the
> opposite sin of conspicuous waste. (*The Dyer's Hand*, p. 234)

Wesker simply omits this theft: his Jessica takes no money.

This, like most of Wesker's changes, gives greater consistency to
the characters. It is difficult to understand how Shakespeare's
modest, thoughtful Jessica could behave with such insensitivity,
but Wesker's Jessica is seen progressing explosively towards her
inconsiderate but honest flight. Shakespeare's Portia is said to be
wise as well as beautiful, as her decisiveness in dealing with
Antonio's trial proves, yet to the less decisive Bassanio she calls
herself 'an unlessoned girl, unschooled, unpractised' whose gentle
spirit 'commits itself to yours to be directed, As from her Lord, her
Governor, her King' (III ii). Wesker's Portia produces her
inspiration about the bond from an educated and trained
intelligence, of which, as a 'New Woman', she is proud. Having
demonstrated her powers, she makes no conventional show of
being subordinate and deferential to Bassanio.

The verbal echoes of Shakespeare in Wesker's play are few:
there is no 'quality of mercy' speech; Bassanio's 'In Belmont is a
lady richly left' (I i) becomes, simply 'In Belmont sir, there is a
lady' (p. 19), for Wesker's Portia has inherited mainly ruins; and
lines from the other famous speech of Shakespeare's play, Shylock's
'Hath not a Jew eyes?' (III i), are spoken by Shylock's opponent,
Lorenzo. Again, the new context creates a new significance, for
what on Shylock's lips is a sincere and powerful plea for equality
becomes, from Lorenzo, a patronising statement of the obvious.

Over the whole play, then, the effect of the changes is clear — it
becomes an indictment of man's inhumanity to man, especially

Jewish man. But many of the technical changes, in language, structure and characterisation, point to the differences between the playwrights and the *kind* of plays they are writing. The greater consistency of the characters in Wesker's play indicates his debt to naturalism: some of his earlier plays dealt fully with the effect of environment and conditions on character, and although he has also written plays in non-naturalistic styles, his continuing interest in the interaction of people and their external circumstances appears in *The Merchant*. Both his Jewish and his Venetian characters appear in several scenes during which the main plot lines are hardly mentioned, simply so that their normal behaviour can be established. In Shakespearean comedy there is more plot, usually turning on arbitrary premises or coincidences which would be unacceptable in a modern play aiming at reflecting 'real life'. At the same time, Wesker's use of the historical setting enables him to make more adventurous use of long speeches and eloquent language which, without being artificial or improbable, are not as limiting as modern everyday speech.

Finally, to the question of whether the play stands alone and can be judged without reference to Shakespeare's original, the answer must be that it is a coherent and valid work in its own right.

Two other modern playwrights have written well-known plays with Shakespeare's as starting points — Tom Stoppard's *Rosencrantz and Guildenstern are dead* based on *Hamlet*, and Edward Bond's *Lear* based on *King Lear*. But where Stoppard's play depends for its effect on our knowing the small role his main characters play in *Hamlet*, Bond's and Wesker's plays rework the whole of their originals into new and self-contained units. This is why Wesker (with Bond) retains so little of Shakespeare's dialogue and why *The Merchant* does not depend directly upon its predecessor.

The Characters

Shylock

It is important to the play that Shylock's positive, energetic, generous qualities are apparent, for there is a major conflict between vitality and the fixed, inflexible systems of law and prejudice. Shylock is in fact a man who is overfull of energy, which can be both a good and a bad thing. From the first we see him saying and doing more than is necessary. Lorenzo calls him 'A loud, enthusiastic man' (p. 27), and his daughter Jessica

complains 'But he bullies with it all' (p. 9). Antonio however
loves him for his energy, and his generosity is evident in more than
financial terms: he is generous with time, money, effort towards
all his friends and guests.

But mixed with his eagerness is a vein of pessimism, apparent in
his references to the cruelties inflicted on his own race, which
epitomise the cruelties of all mankind towards each other.

> I am sometimes horrified by the passion of my contempt for
> men. Can I be so without pity for their stupidities, compassion
> for their frailties, excuses for their cruelties? It is as though
> these books of mine have spoken too much, too long; the
> massacres by kings, the deathly little spites of serfs, the
> oppressive jealousies and hurts of scholars, who had more
> learning than wisdom. Too much, Antonio, too much. Seeing
> what men have done, I know with great weariness the pattern of
> what they will do, and I have such contempt, such contempt it
> bewilders me. (p. 63—64)

Therefore it is in spite of this pessimism that he insists that the
world is in the long term organised according to 'the scheme of
things' — a meaningful, purposeful pattern. Both his natural vitality
and his belief in the scheme of things working for good lead him to
act more incautiously than is wise for a Jew in Venice. His sister
Rivka sums up his wilful optimism as self-deception: 'Pretend,
pretend, pretend! All your life! Wanting to be what you're not.
Imaging the world as you want' (p. 57). Yet his refusal to expect
the worst of mankind is a generous mistake. It is the pressure of
society, embodied in its laws, that finally confirms his pessimism.
Shylock leaves the court defeated in a deeper sense than just that
he has lost the unwanted bond, for he has lost his will to keep
fighting his contempt and believing in the scheme of things.

Tubal

An important aspect of the other male inhabitants of the Ghetto
Nuovo is the range of different personalities they display — they
are a cross-section of a community, and by their varied
temperaments disprove the prejudice that all Jews conform to a
stereotype. Tubal is Shylock's partner and therefore also a
loan-banker, a business man. He is benevolent but more cautious
than Shylock, whom he regards with tolerant affection. His
tolerance means that he imposes no restraint on Shylock,
for though he is wise enough to perceive what is ill-advised in

Shylock's treatment of Jessica, he says nothing, for 'you can't discuss children with parents, you offend them where they've placed their most cherished endeavour' (p. 10). Thus he throws Shylock's character into relief by contrast, and his friendship shows Shylock at home in his own community and demonstrates that Shylock has not needed to befriend Antonio to compensate for being a misfit amongst his own people.

Roderigues
Like Moses and Solomon Usque, Roderigues, the young architect, is a creative person. He shares Shylock's abounding energy – he 'rushes in' (p. 10), and exaggerates: 'I stay up all night . . . All night! . . . Well, not *all* night' (p. 10). He is in love with Jessica, but Shylock dismisses him as 'a sweet boy' (p. 12) and not suitable for Jessica. Roderigues is perceptive enough to see Graziano as 'everyman's everything' (p. 54) and to understand the conflict between Jessica and her father. His frank eagerness contrasts with Jessica's other suitor, the intense Lorenzo.

Moses of Castelazzo
Moses on the other hand is an irascible eighty year-old painter. His is a 'cameo part', a brief apperance in one scene without contributing directly to the plot. His bad temper perhaps reflects his position as a recognised artist, his fame too well established for him to care about it – he provides an astringent element in the friendly, benevolent gathering at Shylock's house.

Solomon Usque
Equally renowned is the playwright Solomon Usque. However, though he is 'self-appointed plenipotentiary for refugees' (p. 14) and travels constantly, evidently to some purpose, his personal manner is unworldly and unsophisticated – 'He's always greeting the wrong person . . . pushing the wrong door . . . drinking from the wrong shaped glass . . . When artists aspire to elegance they end by being ridiculous' (p. 11). He is the kind of artist whose absorption in his work makes him less confident in dealing with other people, unlike Moses. Modest about his own plays, he is also unlike Shylock and Roderigues in avoiding dramatic assertions about the persecution of Jews in Portugal, and this makes his simple list of destructions the more effective.

Antonio

Antonio is the 'merchant' of the title but, as in Shakespeare's play, his part is secondary in importance to Shylock's. On the whole he is a wise, intelligent man, recognising in Shylock's character an adventurousness he admires and envies;

> Those books. Look at them. How they remind me what I am, what I've done. Nothing! A merchant! A purchaser of this to sell there. A buyer up and seller off . . . It never worried me, this absence of curiosity for travel. Until I met you, old Jew (p. 3)

His disillusionment extends to Venetian politics too: 'I've lost my appetite for the intrigues and boredom of administration. I can't pretend this is a city of holiness and light' (p. 74). Yet he has a certain rashness, springing perhaps from his lack of real interest in his trade and social position. He has sent out all his fortune at once ('Insane', Shylock calls it); he agrees to lend Bassanio a lot of money, though he doesn't really trust him, and, after cautiously insisting that Shylock follow the law in making their bond, he finally joins with him in the 'nonsense bond' mocking the law. Like Shylock, who has stepped out of his appointed place in the state to assert his rights as a human being, Antonio has departed from his role as Venetian patrician and merchant: even when threatened with death, he reaffirms his belief in knowledge and curiosity above everything else.

Bassanio

Bassanio, Wesker has said, is

> a confidence trickster . . . Right from the moment of his first encounter with Antonio, when he sees he has made his mistake, he withdraws and does something else. But Antonio can see straight through him. And there's his manipulation of the casket scene. This is when Portia becomes worried about him . . . She embraces him and says, 'Now leave. I must arrange and scheme for you.' And he says, 'I have no words' He's cool, untouched, and at the moment he gives himself away. (*Theatre Quarterly* 28 p. 24)

He is not a criminal, just very self-centred and unscrupulous in pursuing his own interests. It is he who warns Lorenzo against getting too personally involved in his principles — 'Not too far' he says (p. 29). His view of trade and the profit motive is as cynical as Antonio's, but unlike Antonio he is happy that this is so.

His pragmatic views are expressed to his friends: to Antonio, on whom he wants to make a good impression, he professes the contradictory respect for 'Venetian rule of law . . . Her Christian pride and fervour' (p. 40). By the end of the play he has learnt nothing — his complacency about his own superiority remains, seen in his patronising intention that Portia shall be 'cherished but not spoilt' (p. 84).

Lorenzo

Lorenzo is a more complex and perhaps more dangerous character because, though honestly committed to his own beliefs, he is both intolerant and inclined to be fanatical. His fanaticism is negative, and his poetry advocates a return to simplicity that implies the destruction of many aspects of Venetian civilisation, including the toleration of the Jews: 'A nation that confuses timidity for tolerance is a nation without principle' (p. 27). Nonetheless he realises his own confusion between his wish for simplicity, for black and white rules about right and wrong, and his fascination with the politics of power.

> My nature can't decide itself. I feel passionate appetites within me but for what? The fool depresses me yet I myself believe in God enough to risk being called a simpleton. I despise power yet so much offends me that I want power to wipe out the offence. (p. 28).

During the courtroom scene, he shows his skill in oratory to 'make capital' politically, as the doge puts it, out of Antonio's predicament, and even appears to be defending Shylock, 'flooding the proceedings with conciliatory warmth and charm' (p. 76), in order to make his political attack on those in power whom he really wants to see blamed for the crisis. In fact, his religious beliefs mean that he is less tolerant towards Shylock than he pretends, and his true position is tactlessly explained to Jessica — all Jews, including herself, are 'of a forsaken race, married to a God they'd thought had chosen them. Doomed!' (p. 67). And with the same complacent superiority as Bassanio, he plans to alter Jessica's life and beliefs to suit himself. As Jessica says: without tolerance, humility and a sense of perspective, 'his strength is arrogance, his seriousness is pedantry, his devotion is frenzy' (p. 68).

Graziano

Antonio describes Graziano before he appears as one who

'manifests the most depressingly boisterous happiness I know'
(p. 15). It is his superficiality rather than his boisterousness that
makes him despicable however — he 'bends so with the wind,
quickly rushing to agree with the next speaker' (p. 15). In the
warehouse scene this eagerness to agree and to retract as soon as
contradicted, like his admitted foolishness, makes him a familiar
comic character, the silly young man who makes amusing mistakes.
But his superficiality has its dangerous side, in his uncritical
adoption of the common hostility against the Jews, both casually
in his mockery of Tubal and in his unthinking exclamations in the
court: 'A plot! A plot! A Jewish plot!' (p. 74) With perhaps
improbable cynicism he sums up his role in the last scene: 'There's
a lot to be said for a sycophant! (p. 83).

The Doge

Of the other characters, only the doge has a speaking part.
Personally, he is shrewd; witness his swiftness to check Lorenzo's
self-advertising propaganda; and he is equally swift to check, with a
veiled threat, Antonio's sneer at his own patrician privilege — 'But
do not strain it, friend. Do not' (p. 80). His small role as judge in
the trial scene conveys the authority of Venetian government —
when he is not asking necessary questions of the participants, he
expounds the political and legal situation in clear, unqualified,
absolute statements, reflecting the inflexibility of the laws that are
being invoked.

Jessica

Jessica is like her father Shylock in having an assertive personality,
and this personality has developed partly in reaction against him.
His enthusiasms tend to overwhelm people, and Jessica objects to
this, feeling her individuality being crushed. Her dissatisfaction and
frustration lead her to reject Shylock's values of scholarship,
learning, order, meaning — 'the scheme of things'. She fears that
life is not meaningful: 'I do not believe that there is a scheme of
things, only chaos and misery . . . and in it we must carve out just
sufficient order for an ounce of happiness' (p. 9). She would
thus see her escape from family duties to happiness with Lorenzo
as justified. It is only after they flee to Belmont that she finds that
the ounce of happiness is not enough to outweigh the other values
that Lorenzo expects her to discard. She is also honest and
affectionate, as her outspoken defence of Shylock both at Belmont
and in the Venetian courtroom show, and by the last scene she has

obviously decided she prefers her established affections and
loyalties to Lorenzo's fanaticism. Her role in the play forms an
interesting contrast with Portia's — both are the well-educated
daughters of fathers who exercise injudicious control over them,
but equally unsatisfactory results follow from Portia's obedience
and Jessica's disobedience.

Rivka

Shylock's wise sister is as warm-hearted and generous as he is, but
more cautious. She understands and is concerned for him:

> Oh Shylock, my young brother, I've watched you, wandering
> away from Jewish circles, putting your nose out in alien places.
> I've watched you be restless and pretend you can walk in
> anybody's streets. Don't think I've not understood you;
> suffocating in this little yard, waiting for your very own scholar
> to arrive. It made me ache to watch you . . . (p. 57).

Without being as embittered as Shylock and Jessica eventually
become, she has fewer illusions about the society they live in. As a
mother-figure to Jessica, without a mother's power to affect the
father-daughter relationship, she tries to moderate the attitudes of
both.

Rebecca da Mendes

Rebecca is something of a great lady in her community, her father
having been a banker 'renowned' for his 'benevolence' (p. 11).
Like Usque, who acts as her escort, she is travelling as a kind of
ambassador for the Jewish families escaping from persecution in
Portugal, and thus has a responsible position. Her small part in the
play adds to the array of intelligent and effective female characters,
and shows that the controls that Jessica and Portia are threatened
with by fathers and husbands are not inescapable.

Portia

Portia is a strong character, although she enters the main action
late in the play. She is a 'New Woman' of the Renaissance, one of
the few who, like Queen Elizabeth the First of England, whom she
mentions, has been released by the revival of classical learning from
the traditionally limited place of women. She catalogues her own
powers:

> Yes, she can spin, weave, sew. Give her meat and drink — she
> can dress them. Show her flax and wool — she can make you

clothes. But — Portia reads! Plato and Aristotle, Ovid and
Catullus, all in the original! Latin, Greek, Hebrew . . . She has
read history and politics, she has studied logic and mathematics,
astronomy and geography, she has conversed with liberal minds
on the nature of the soul, the efficacy of religious freedom, the
very existence of God! (p. 48)

Thus she is in her way an equivalent of Shylock in her wide
interests — and also in her energy, inherited from her peasant
mother. Her claims to both intelligence and energy appear in the
decisive outlines of her plans:

I shall raise what I can from the sale of our properties . . . We
must reclaim the land . . . Timber is scarce, the number of ships
registered by Venice is dropping. Signs, my dear, the signs are
there . . . The land! I've decided! (p. 45—46)

Her energy is based on the belief that 'The material things of this
world count. We have no soul without labour' (p. 46). Where
Shylock is brought down by the inflexible pressure of the law,
Portia's career is hampered by her dead father's choice of a
husband for her. Her early exuberance — 'I could found cities with
my strengths' (p. 52) — comes up against Bassanio's conventional
limitations and the unimaginative narrowness of the Venetian legal
system. In the last scene Antonio still sees her as 'blossoming with
purpose' but her purposes have become less exuberant: she will
'dutifully take my role of wife' though 'I am to be reckoned with,
you know, not merely dutiful' (p. 84). She, like Shylock, can
only act within the limits that society prescribes for her, and when
she says 'something in me has died struggling to grow up' (p. 84),
she has realised that her life is not going to be an adventure but a
fight against adversity.

Nerissa

Though Nerissa is Portia's maid, she is not merely a servant — her
position is nearer that of the 'waiting-gentlewoman' in many of
Shakespeare's plays, combining the role of companion,
housekeeper and secretary. An early arranged marriage such as hers
was more usual in the upper ranges of society than the lower, and
she seems to have become Portia's 'maid' because of the 'miseries
of an ill-chosen marriage'. So in conversation, though she addresses
Portia as 'my lady' and 'madam', she is frank and unconstrained,
teasing her and advising her where necessary; she also offers
suggestions unasked, as 'Why don't *you* attend the court in Venice,

madam?' (p. 69). However, she is not emotionally involved in the
bond plot herself, so that in the final scene, while Portia, Jessica
and Antonio stand aside in their melancholy, she can act as
detached observer, satirising the young men as 'Heroes'.

Language and style

'I'd have been mad to go into competition with Shakespeare as a
poet!' (*Theatre Quarterly* 28 p. 24) Wesker said, and so, as in all his
plays, he wrote in prose. He was not trying to construct a
pseudo-Elizabethan idiom, nor did he use aggressively modern
language:

> Someone who read the script said it sounded very Victorian,
> which was interesting because I had been doing a lot of work on
> Ruskin at the same time, and reading a lot in the Victorian
> novelists. (*TQ* 28 p. 24)

He was not, of course, aiming at a nineteenth-century style — this
impression is created because the dialogue, without being archaic,
is more formal than most modern speech. An audience accepts
formal speech from characters in historical setting and costume:
the characters are obviously living in a different environment from
that of twentieth-century man, and it is reasonable that their
speech should be different too. Therefore Wesker felt able to write
dialogue which has more pattern and formality than the casual
conversation of the present day. Thus when Portia says —

> My mother taught love ripens on the mind, is made of passions,
> laughter, all the minutiae of living shared rather than surmised.
> Is that pedantic, you think? Would you rather I embrace you
> now and say, with routine ardour, that *your* choice decides?
> (p. 51)

— her vocabulary ('minutiae', 'surmised') draws on a range of
precise words, and her image of love ripening on the mind, like a
fruit, is striking without being pretentiously poetic. There is a
definite pattern in the exchange between Antonio and Shylock,
extending to more than a page of text, an exchange which is simple
and to the point, but contains repetitions that are unobtrusive yet
are sustained just a little more elaborately than in naturalistically
unstructured conversation — the initial 'I knows' of their discussion,
followed by a pause, lead to a variation — 'I understand':

> SHYLOCK. I'm frightened that you don't.
> ANTONIO. I do.

> SHYLOCK. I will not bend the law.
> ANTONIO. I understand.

And this brings them back to the refrain of knowing:

> SHYLOCK. I must not set a precedent.
> ANTONIO. I know.
> SHYLOCK. *You* said. *You* taught.
> ANTONIO. Shylock, Shylock. I'm not afraid.
> SHYLOCK. Oh friend! What have I done to you? (*Pause*.)

This series of short interchanges is completed by a similar but more extended passage that ends with the previous moment of reassurance-then-anguish reversed to anguish-then-reassurance:

> ANTONIO. . . . We shall both be put to death.
> SHYLOCK. I know.
> ANTONIO. I by you. You by them.
> SHYLOCK. I know, I know.
> ANTONIO. We know, we know! We keep saying we know so
>   much.
> SHYLOCK. Gently, gently, dear friend, I'm not afraid either.
>   (pp. 62–63)'

At the other extreme there are long speeches, such as Shylock's very long exposition of how classical learning survived the dark ages. Of a similar long speech about scientific discoveries in his play *The Friends*. Wesker had added a note: 'It is of paramount importance that the actor make as much sense of this précis as possible while at the same time clowning the story' (Wesker, *Volume Three*, p. 101), and here Shylock 'tells his story with mounting excitement and theatricality' — the theatrical dimension is essential in presenting the text, but the text itself is theatrical in style, in that statements are varied with exclamations and questions expressing Shylock's enthusiasm about the subject:

> *What* a work! What a faith! But why? Why should he have
> bothered? What makes one man so cherish the work of others
> that he lovingly guards it, copies, preserves it? And a Christian,
> too, preserving the works of pagans! I love it! (p. 42)

Most of Shylock's speeches are full of these characteristic exclamations and questions, suggesting his enthusiastic, enquiring personality. Graziano too has an individual style, as his stupidity leads him to comic hesitations:

> Least of all I. Me. Least of all me. Or is it 'I'? (p. 29).

Other characters are distinguished by less evident
individualisation of tone and content; such as Jessica's
uncompromising assertions, Tubal's wise, moderate qualifications
of others' extremism (so many of his sentences begin with 'but'),
or Bassanio's wary, concessive use of tentative forms of speech —
'may', 'perhaps', 'sometimes', 'surely'.

One of the objections initially levelled against the script was
that the characters 'say what they mean' — not that they are too
honest, as characters, but that they are unnaturally articulate: thus
Portia describes herself fully and frankly, and we are expected to
take her account as reliable. This, however, like the little
preliminary descriptions of Graziano and Lorenzo, is a convention
of traditional comedy, including Shakespearian comedy, and
Wesker has borrowed this explicitness along with the more formal
language.

In fact Wesker has always included a certain number of long,
carefully structured speeches, many of them giving a character's
self-revelation, even in his modern naturalistic plays, and it is
simply that there are more of them, needing less careful
preparation — or disguise — in *The Merchant*. Shylock's long
speech on 'contempt' forms a general insight into his character, as
does Antonio's exposition of his belief in education during the trial
scene. Some of the actors in the American production questioned
the probability of such a theoretical subject being expounded at a
point when Antonio was in danger of his life, and Wesker was
persuaded to add the line 'Yes. Even at such an hour I remember
these things' (p. 73), but to some extent this apology is not
necessary because Antonio's testimony explains his situation at
that very moment — 'why I bind my fate to Shylock, what I see
in him' (p. 72) — and the length and expansiveness of that
explanation is in keeping with the generally more elaborate
language of the play as a whole.

Themes

Obviously one of the main themes of *The Merchant* is the evil
effect of anti-semitism in Venice as elsewhere, but it is only one
strand in a group of themes all illustrating 'man's inhumanity to
man'. The anti-semitism is at one level an example of an unthinking
hostility towards any noticeably alien individual or minority group.
The Royal Shakespeare Company's 1971 programme for *The*

Merchant of Venice comments on this common hostility:

> A black American, James Baldwin, has defined the scapegoat
> principle as the absolute need 'to discover, or invent . . . the
> stranger, the barbarian, who is responsible for our confusion
> and our pain. Once he is driven out — destroyed — then we can
> be at peace.'

Thus in many societies, there are and have been witch-hunts, either
literally when old women are blamed for bad harvests or disease, or
metaphorically as Senator McCarthy's searching out of American
communists in the 1950s, or in periods of high unemployment,
when immigrants (predominantly those who can be easily
recognised as such by colour or accent) are accused of 'taking away
our jobs'. Shylock describes this scapegoat principle as it affects
his society:

> Jew! Jew, Jew, Jew! I hear the name around and everywhere.
> Your wars go wrong, the Jew must be the cause of it; your
> economic systems crumble, there the Jew must be; your wives
> get sick of you — a Jew will be an easy target for your sour
> frustrations. Failed university, professional blunderings,
> self-loating — the Jew, the Jew, the cause the Jew. (p. 77)

Society is condemning the Jews as a group, *en masse,* not as
individuals. The individualism which makes Shylock reject such
generalisations is termed by Wesker the 'Free Spirit'. When asked
to define his Shylock in a word, as Hamlet might be defined by
indecision or Lear by foolish old age, Wesker wrote:

> I'd never thought of him in a word. Being a vain playwright
> I'd always imagined my Shylock to be too arrestingly complex,
> too contradictory to be held down by one work or phrase. But
> . . . suddenly it came to me: my Shylock was a free spirit. That's
> what he was about, and that's what I was about, and that, I
> realised, is what Jewishness is about. ('The Two Roots of
> Judaism' — a paper for the Rockefeller Foundation Conference,
> Bellagio, Italy, 1982)

This theme of the free spirit is crucial to the conflict of the play,
most clearly in Shylock's role:

> He refuses to accept the constricting spiritual as well as physical
> walls of the Ghetto, and claims a Christian for a friend. Who
> does he think he is? . . . He invents a mocking bond for a pound
> of flesh. He wants to mock them! Who does he think he is? And

he's arrogant with it all. Not only does he talk to Antonio as an equal but he's contemptuous of Antonio's young guests, especially the fanatical Lorenzo, with whom he refuses to engage in debate; and when he does, he tells *them* how to read the history of *their own* state! Really, who does he think he is? ('The Two Roots of Judaism')

Wesker goes on, 'Well, we know who he thinks he is. Foolishly he thinks he's a free spirit', and emphasises that the theme is not limited to Shylock:

> The free spirit implies the supremacy of the human being over the state, over repressive authority, over that which aims to frustrate initiative, cripple imagination, induce conformity. Shylock embodies all of this . . . ('The Two Roots of Judaism')

Jessica's and Portia's oppression by their loving fathers and their would-be manipulation by their would-be husbands is similarly a frustration of their free spirit, based on a general idea of what is suitable for women, as daughters and wives. Thus, simple human relationships such as that of parent and child, or friendship — important themes in most of Wesker's plays — are here distorted by outside pressures. Wesker is saying that the bonds of custom, convention and tradition that affect such relationships are to blame — not personal ill-will on the part of the characters.

These social bonds are like the more formal laws of Venice which prove Shylock's undoing, and Wesker found himself becoming more interested in the theme of 'barbaric laws' — inasmuch as any laws are likely to prove too hard and fast in many cases. The law does not take into account good or bad motives, the circumstances, changing attitudes; Portia's complaint about the law's inflexibility explains its destructiveness:

> I grow. Why can't they? What *I* thought yesterday might be wrong today. What should I do? Stand by my yesterdays because I have made them? I made today as well! And tomorrow, that I'll make too, and all my days, as my intelligence demands. (p. 81)

And Shylock concludes bitterly,

> Take my books. The law must be observed. We have need of the law, what need do we have of books? Distressing, disturbing things, besides. Why, dear friend, they'd even make us question laws. (p. 81)

The letter of the law, as in Shakespeare's play, is destructive without the spirit of justice, but, as Wesker's Portia comments 'The law is not to do with justice' (p. 69).

By comparison, the theme of money is of less importance in *The Merchant,* except inasmuch as it underlies the issue of usury. Portia is only potentially rich, and her stress on 'material things' shows her interest in the real world around her rather than in money for its own sake. Shylock himself is casual and generous with money, and it is not the need for money, ultimately, that puts him and Antonio in danger of their lives — it is their joint flouting of the majesty of the law.

Knowledge, learning and education on the other hand are positive values to set against the rigidity of law and society. As Shylock suggests in his after dinner speech, and as Antonio asserts in the courtroom, knowledge is valued by many kinds of men over many generations, and it grows and changes as mankind does. However, Bassanio, Graziano and Lorenzo are all well educated without being truly enlightened, and the Renaissance society of Venice, in spite of its inheritance of classical learning, still uses mean laws to apply its unenlightened prejudices. So Shylock's loss of his books symbolises his loss of the more optimistic attitude with which the play opened. Yet Wesker uses the last scene to re-establish a note of hope. Even though the young Venetians are as uncharitable, complacent and imperceptive as ever, Antonio and Portia look to the future, people of goodwill, prepared to go on as best they may in the light of their greater humanity.

Performance

The Merchant was first produced in Stockholm, Sweden, where the theatre has a special relationship with Arnold Wesker, then in America in New York, and the British premiere took place at the Birmingham Repertory Theatre in October 1978. Originally the National Theatre in London rejected the script; Peter Hall, the director, and his colleagues felt that too much had been put into the play. However people who had been involved in earlier plays by Wesker indicated their interest — Eddie Kulukundis, the producer who had financed *The Friends,* and, most important, John Dexter, the director of Wesker's first five plays. Wesker noted:

> Have just been to the National . . . it was while talking to Peter that I turned and saw a beaming John Dexter. He opened his arms and we embraced. Damn him, he's irresistible for me, I

suppose. Surely I've said this before, but he's a first love. He
directed my first five plays, and they were his first five. Within
seconds he was saying: 'I've read *The Merchant* and isn't it
good. It's very good indeed.' (Diary)

Now Dexter's prestige was such that he could influence theatre
managements, especially with Kulukundis' backing: 'Eddie had said
he'd open it at The National (Hall would let a Dexter direct it)'
(Diary). But Dexter himself at that time was disillusioned with the
National Theatre, and enthusiastic about opening in New York,
with Shylock played by the actor Zero Mostel, then internationally
famous as the star of the stage musical, *Fiddler on the Roof.*

Wesker likes to participate in the rehearsals of his plays, seeing
the first production as a kind of final draft of his work, but his
presence during the American rehearsals meant that he was under
pressure to make any changes that other people wanted, even
against his own better judgement. Heated argument, for instance,
about Shylock's ability actually to kill a friend with his knife drove
Wesker into an embattled defence:

'You're talking about another kind of play. My play is about
"barbaric laws, barbaric bonds", simply that. That's all I want
to explore . . . Now, you want a play about what happens when
a man actually has to kill his friend. What does he do? I didn't
think about it this way when I was writing but I now see that I
instinctively avoided what I felt I could not honestly handle. I
don't know what Shylock would do — nor what I would do —
and so I didn't let the situation get that far. I use Shakespeare's
device and bring on Portia. Fault me for that but that's the play
I want to write.' (Diary)

He was less able to defend his lines from the cuts that the
management demanded, for the sake of reducing the play to a
more conventional commercial length. This led to conflict when
Dexter, acting on the management's behalf, went ahead with cuts,
and Wesker finally complained: 'I wanted to write an epic, now it's
neat, Reader's Digest' (Diary).

Wesker has had personal bad luck with the openings of several
of his plays — his father died on the first night of *The Kitchen,* his
mother on the first night of the Swedish *Merchant* — and this time
Zero Mostel died suddenly after the first preview night in
Philadelphia. This shock and the disruption of the production
upset everyone. The play continued with Mostel's understudy as
Shylock, but it was not a success on Broadway, where the

influential *New York Times* critic concluded 'the evening is stimulating but only sometimes successful'.

Many other American reviewers were very impressed with the play, and those who didn't like it tended to concentrate on what they saw as the temerity of 'rewriting Shakespeare'. In Britain on the other hand no critics were shocked. The tradition of re-interpreting and rewriting Shakespeare already has a respectable pedigree. Yet in spite of critical praise such as 'a double and totally unexpected triumph', 'a compelling play' and 'a mighty work', the British production never transferred from Birmingham, and still has not been performed in London.

Further reading

Wesker's Work
Most of Wesker's plays have been published by Jonathan Cape:
The Kitchen, 1961
The Wesker Trilogy, 1960, which contains *Chicken Soup With
    Barley*, *Roots* and *I'm Talking About Jerusalem*
Chips With Everything, 1962
The Four Seasons, 1966
Their Very Own and Golden City, 1966
The Friends, 1970
The Old Ones, 1973
Caritas, 1981

There is also a four-volume complete paperback edition of the
plays published by Penguin:
Wesker Vols. I, II, III & IV 1979–80

Further books of essays, lectures and short stories available in
paperback are:
Journey into Journalism, 1977
Love Letters on Blue Paper and other stories, 1980

Background reading
Mid-Century Drama by Laurence Kitchin (1960) – contains an
    interview with Wesker, as well as a chapter on his work
Arnold Wesker by Harold U. Ribalow (New York, 1965) –
    Twayne's English Author Series
Anger and After by John Russell Taylor (revised edition, 1969) –
    includes Wesker's plays in a chapter on 'Productions Out of
    Town'
Theatre at Work edited by Charles Marowitz and Simon Trussler
    (1967) – contains a long interview with Wesker
Arnold Wesker by Ronald Hayman (1970) – Contemporary
    Playwrights Series
Arnold Wesker by Glenda Leeming (1972) – Writers and their

Work Series

Theatre Language: a Study of Arden, Osborne, Pinter and Wesker
by John Russell Brown (1972)

Stages in the Revolution by Catherine Itzin (1980) — includes a
chapter on Wesker's political beliefs and position

Wesker the Playwright by Glenda Leeming (1983) — a chapter by
chapter analysis of Wesker's plays written with his own
co-operation

The Merchant

THE MERCHANT

A play in two acts

This is the eighth draft of the play, based on the Birmingham production of 1978, and differs from the version world premiered in Stockholm in 1976 and the English-speaking version premiered on Broadway in 1977. It has been further revised for this edition including the re-ordering of certain scenes.

Dedicated to

my students in the 'contemporary drama' class of Boulder's Summer School in the University of Colorado, U.S.A., with whom I began thinking aloud on this play.

And in particular to:

LOIS BUELER

who not only produced evidence to vindicate my approach to the work but also provided me with a prop upon which its argument stands.

'I do not use despair, for it is not mine,
only entrusted to me for safe-keeping.'
Wislawa Szymborska,
Polish poetess

Acknowledgements

I have always depended upon my friends for comments and criticisms of early drafts of my plays but with *The Merchant* my gratitude also extends to many scholars whose works provided the background to a period and setting I only barely knew.

Of those friends and scholars three must be mentioned for my especial debts. Dr. D.S. Chambers, lecturer in Renaissance Studies at the Warburg Institute, who read the third draft and made many helpful observations, and whose book *The Imperial Age of Venice* I continually raided. Similarly the books of the late Dr. Cecil Roth whose *History of the Jews* everywhere-all-the-time must be invaluable for any creative writer in need of Jewish historical detail. Lastly, the incredible persistence and patience of my friend and German translator, Nina Adler, whose scrupulous intelligence questioned so much that some of the logic and fine detail of the play would not have been as clear without her.

None other of my works have acknowledged such debts — perhaps they should have — but that this one does I'd like taken as a measure of how real and not merely polite this acknowledgement is.

A.W.

Preface

(This article first appeared in the *Guardian*, 29 August 1981)

Once again *The Merchant of Venice* is on school syllabuses. Productions are being mounted around the country. The Royal Shakespeare Company has transferred its version from Stratford to London, though not without some anxiety. Its programme is full of extracts from good and eager Jews with eager good nature defending Shakespeare's humanity and poetry, pointing as always to Shylock's special pleading for his existence — 'Hath not a Jew eyes?' — and carefully getting the play into historical perspective, quite oblivious to the irony in their forgiving the creation of an unforgiving Jew.

Not that their gentle arguments — and bless them! — will stay a few hotheads in the Jewish community from demanding the play be banned from the stage and withdrawn from the school syllabus. But the majority of the Jewish community, if they know what's good for them, will keep quiet. I can't. I have never known what's good for me.

I revere Shakespeare, am proud to write in his shadow, the world is inconceivable without him and I would passionately defend the right of anyone anywhere to present and teach this play. But nothing will make me admire it, nor has anyone persuaded me the holocaust is irrelevant to my responses. Try though I do to listen only to the poet's lines, yet I find myself seething at his portrait of a Jew, unable to pretend this is simply another Shakespearean character through whom he is exploring greed, or whatever.

No character is chosen arbitrarily by a writer, but for his embodiment of the characteristics the writer wishes to set in opposition to other characteristics. The Jew in Shakespeare's play is meant to embody what he wishes to despise. That he gives Shylock lines with which to defend and explain himself has more to do with his dramatic instinct for not making the opposition too black, which would lessen credibility and impact, than it has to do with a wish to be kind to a poor Jew.

There is no evidence anywhere else that Shakespeare was distressed by anti-Jewish feeling. The portrayal of Shylock offends for being a lie about the Jewish character. I seek no pound of flesh but, like Shylock, I'm unforgiving, unforgiving of the play's contribution to the world's astigmatic view and murderous hatred of the Jew.

I ceased finally to be a 'forgiver' when, in 1973, watching Laurence Olivier's oi-yoi-yoi portrayal of Shylock in Jonathan Miller's production at The National Theatre, I was struck by the play's irredeemable anti-semitism. It was not an intellectual evaluation but the immediate impact I actually experienced.

Here was a play which, despite the poetic genius of its author — or who knows, perhaps because of it! — could emerge as nothing other than a confirmation of the Jew as bloodsucker. Worse, the so-called defence of Shylock — 'If you prick him doth he not bleed' — was so powerful that it dignified the anti-semitism. An audience, it seemed to me on that night, could come away with its prejudices about the Jew confirmed but held with an easy conscience because they thought they'd heard a noble plea for extenuating circumstances.

All the productions I've seen of *The Merchant of Venice* have failed to hide the message which insists on coming through clearly and simply. No matter with what heavy tragedy the actor plays the role, no matter how thuggishly or foolishly the Venetians are portrayed, no matter in what setting — such as Miller's Victorian capitalism to show how everyone was involved in filthy money — the image comes through inescapably: the Jew is mercenary and revengeful, sadistic, without pity.

Nothing will move him from that court with his knife which, to show how cruel he really is, he sharpens on his leather before the assembly. Anybody who conceives of such retribution deserves to be spat upon. It is no wonder Antonio treated him as he did — 'many a time and oft, in the Rialto' — for contained within this arrogant and avaricious man were the seeds of the awful bond. Antonio must have seen it. After all, they demanded the Lord's flesh.

How can it surprise us that this bitter, spitting, conniving and mean little alien in the ghetto of Venice would want a pound of flesh from one of its citizens? Neither in Miller's production, nor in any I've ever seen, could I recognise a Jew I knew. Is being spat upon a reasonable extenuating circumstance for extorting such a savagely conceived death? Shylock is revengeful and insists upon his pound of flesh against all humanity and reason. It is a hateful, ignorant portrayal.

On the other hand perhaps it is impossible to think straight about *The Merchant of Venice*. The holocaust could be viewed as the ball and chain to all attempts at reason. There are only a few positions to take and each of them is bound to be unnatural.

There are those Christians who are determined not to be intimidated by the history of Jewish persecution throughout the centuries and who, like John Barton, the director of the RSC's current production, will go looking for other themes — 'true and false value,' he says in a programme note. And there will be those Jews who will bend over backwards to show how just and tolerant they are. The intelligent Chaim Bermant (gratefully quoted in the RSC programme note) explained in *The Jewish Chronicle* (6 March, 1981) that the play 'is a product of its time . . . and in the circumstances his (Shakespeare's) vision of Shylock verges on the sympathetic.'

I don't understand the logic of that argument. If we are presenting the play in 'our times' what is the relevance of pointing out it was a sympathetic vision in past times? We're not living in those times. The vision of Shylock may have been sympathetic then but by no stretch of the imagination can it be viewed as sympathetic now, and anyone producing the play must honestly acknowledge that fact.

'I doubt if *The Merchant of Venice* could induce anti-Jewish feeling in someone who was not already an anti-semite . . .' Bermant continues. Maybe. But it confirms and feeds those whose anti-semitism is latent, dormant. And I would hesitate before suggesting those are an insignificant minority.

It's not only the portrayal of Shylock which offends me. I don't share the bard's sympathetic view of Portia, and it's foolish of those seeking to whitewash the play to say Shakespeare made her a silly girl. She is not meant to be. She's meant to be a heroine, beautiful and wise and generous, and Bassanio is meant to be handsome and dashing, and Antonio is meant to be attractively melancholy.

But what must we think of Portia, who, in spite of possessing knowledge of the one interpretation of the law which will save Antonio his anguish and Shylock his humiliation withholds it and

prattles on about 'the quality of mercy' which she appears
incapable of extending? And what seriousness must we give to
Antonio's melancholy and Bassanio's romantic love when they and
those other stupid people drone on about love and fidelity and
rings who've just witnessed the destruction of a man?

And how lovely Barton makes them in his production, dressed
in white, the night gone, early morning birds, a new day dawning
for them. And with what glee and satisfaction the audience laughed
when Graziano baited Shylock and when finally he was told he
must become a Christian. There's real justice for you.

Barton's production goes one better than most. We will ignore
the silly *Fiddler-On-The-Roof* rendering of the daughter, Jessica,
and her possession of an absurd accent which miraculously her
father seems to have lost! We will ignore that Shylock is placed
in a setting with scales weighing his silver and gold, just in case one
misunderstands the nature of his calling or forgets how he spends
his time.

But what we can't ignore is the moment when Shylock, in pain
that his daughter and jewels have gone, confronts his friend, Tubal,
and cries out '. . . and I know not what's spent in the search . . .'
— at which the canny old Tubal presents him with a bill. Ho! Ho!
The audience laughed again to be reminded that not only do Jews
suck dry Christian blood, they suck each other's as well! Of course!
Jews are insensitive to each other's pain. A debt after all is a debt.
Why wait till grief is past?

Barton's production echoes the play's contemptibility very
clearly and cleanly. You can hear every word, each action is clearly
defined, all motivation cleanly charted. He even seduced the
brilliant actor David Suchet, himself Jewish, into re-creating our
comfortable and reassuring image of the bent old man, his trousers
too long for him, an ever-present false and fawning smile on his
face, grimacing through smoke from an uncouthly hanging cigarillo.

Only Suchet's two marvellous moments endow the character
with wit and dignity. When Portia asks '. . . which is the merchant
here and which the Jew?' the difference is so obvious — Antonio a
tall upright Aryan, Shylock stooped, dark and diminutive — that
Suchet releases a huge, mischievous laugh at the crassness of the
question. And at the end, forced to confront the oppressiveness of
the state and his self-inflicted humiliation, Suchet's face reveals a
despair which has more to do with concentration camps than
anything we've seen till now. In fact his eyes betray the play.

It was while watching the Jonathan Miller production in 1973

that I first began to think of alternative'. When the moment
came for Portia to announce that Shylock couldn't have his pound
of flesh because it meant spilling blood which was not called for in
the contract, I was struck with an insight. The real Shylock would
not have torn his hair out and raged against not being allowed to
cut his pound of flesh, but would have said 'Thank God!' The
point of writing a play in which Shylock would utter these words
would be to explain how he became involved in such a bond in the
first place.

My first note to myself was that Shylock and Antonio must be
friends. My second was that Shylock must be a bibliophile.
Gradually, as I researched the history of the Venetian Empire, of
the Jews in Italy, of the development of printing – of the entire
Renaissance in fact – I realised that my play would not be about
bonds for usury but about bonds of friendship and the state laws
which could threaten that friendship.

My version of the story – *The Merchant* – opens in the Jewish
Ghetto of Venice, and what an exciting, lively place that was by
1563. Ghetto Nuovo is the old Venetian word for 'new
iron-foundry,' which is where the Jews – needed but not wanted –
were pushed aside to live on the outskirts of Venice. (And from
that moment the word entered the world's vocabulary to denote an
ethnic slum. The Ghetto Nuovo exists to this day.)

The first scene of the play establishes the relationship, evokes
the period. It takes place in Shylock's study, strewn with books
and manuscripts. Shylock, a 'loan-banker,' and his friend Antonio,
a merchant, are leisurely cataloguing. They are old friends, and old;
in their middle sixties.

But how could such friends enter into an absurd bond for a
pound of flesh? Research showed that no dealings could be entered
into with a Jew without contract. This becomes one of the pillars
later on in the play. Antonio needs to borrow three thousand
ducats to lend to his godson. Shylock would prefer to give him the
money, but Antonio points out that the laws of Venice do not
permit this.

The familiar tragedy unfolds. Antonio loses his ships, and
Shylock is faced with a quite new dilemma which is spelt out to
him by Rivka, his sister:

'Don't you know the court will relieve you of your bond to save
a citizen's life? . . . They will even let you bend the law and lend
him further ducats for repayment when the hour is passed . . . But
not everyone in the Ghetto will agree to the bending of the law,

will they? And that's where your moral problem begins. You can't
see that? . . . Some may. Some may even beg you to do that rather
than have the blood of a Christian on their hands. But others will
say, no! Having bent the law for us, how often will they bend it for
themselves and then we'll live in even greater uncertainties than
before. They'll be divided, as you are, my clever brother. Who to
save — your poor people or your poor friend? You can't see that?'

The play ends in court. Shylock has no alternative but to
safeguard his community and sacrifice his friend and, consequently,
himself. Portia comes to the rescue but the state exacts its revenge.
He must not merely lose his house goods but his beloved collection
of books, in which he has enthusiastically claimed resides the
world's wisdom. He's a destroyed man.

Shylock has entered the language. To be called it is to be
insulted for being mean like a Jew. A director of Hungarian origin
told me he'd seen a production in war-time Hungary where the
play's anti-semitic aspects were inevitably exploited to the hilt.
Jessica was portrayed as a whore. I can't help feeling there's a
certain honesty to such a production, and I would like to think
Shakespeare today would be ashamed of his contribution to the
world's image of that poor, old battered race.

The poet in him is untouchable but I know about Jewish ghetto
life, and history has a hindsight which I felt driven to use. All my
play offers is a new set of evidence from which a theatre public
may choose.

The Merchant received its world premiere at the Royal Dramaten-theater, Stockholm, on 8 October 1976, directed by Staphan Roos.

It received its English-speaking premiere at the Plymouth Theatre, New York, on 16 November 1977, with the following cast.

SHYLOCK KOLNER	Joseph Leon
JESSICA	Julie Garfield
RIVKA	Marian Seldes
TUBAL DI PONTI	John Seitz
ANTONIO QUERINI	John Clements
BASSANIO VISCONTI	Nicolas Surovy
LORENZO PISANI	Everett McGill
GRAZIANO SANUDO	Riggs O'Hara
PORTIA CONTARINI	Roberta Maxwell
NERISSA	Gloria Gifford
SOLOMON USQUE	Jeffrey Horowitz
REBECCA DA MENDES	Angela Wood
MOSES OF CASTELAZZO	Leib Lensky
GIROLAMO PRIULI	William Roerick
ABTALION DA MODENA	Boris Tumarin
MAID/SINGER	Rebecca Malka
SERVANTS/SENATORS	Russ Banham
	Mark Blum
	Philip Carroll
	James David Cromar
	Brian Meister
	John Tyrrell

Directed by John Dexter
Designed by Jocelyn Herbert
Lighting by Andy Phillips

N.B. Zero Mostel was originally cast as Shylock but tragically he died after the first night out of town in Philadelphia — 8 September 1977.

The Merchant received its British premiere at the Birmingham Repertory Theatre on 12 October 1978, with the following cast.

SHYLOCK KOLNER	David Swift
JESSICA	Julia Swift
RIVKA	Hana Maria Pravda
TUBAL DI PONTI	Aubrey Morris
ANTONIO QUERINI	Frank Middlemass
BASSANIO VISCONTI	Tim Hardy
LORENZO PISANI	Greg Hicks
GRAZIANO SANUDO	Timothy Spall
PORTIA CONTARINI	Angela Down
NERISSA	Margi Campi
RODERIGUES DE CUNHA	Teddy Kempner
SOLOMON USQUE	Roger Allam
REBECCA DA MENDES	Judith Harte
MOSES OF CASTELAZZO	Alfred Hoffmann
GIROLAMO PRIULI	Andre Van Gyseghem
MAID/SINGER	Joanna Foster
SERVANTS/SENATORS	Peter Evans
	Christopher Gillespie
	Ian McFarlane
	Raymond Savage

Directed by Peter Farago
Sets designed by Christopher Morley
Costumes designed by Ann Curtis
Lighting by Mick Hughes

CHARACTERS

SHYLOCK KOLNER, *a Jew of Venice*

JESSICA, *his daughter*

RIVKA, *his sister*

TUBAL DI PONTI, *his partner*

ANTONIO QUERINI, *a merchant of Venice*

BASSANIO VISCONTI, *his godson*

LORENZO PISANI, *Bassanio's friend*

GRAZIANO SANUDO, *Antonio's assistant*

PORTIA CONTARINI, *an heiress of Venice*

NERISSA, *her maid*

RODERIGUES DE CUNHA, *an architect*

SOLOMON USQUE, *a playwright*

REBECCA DA MENDES, *daughter of Portuguese banker*

MOSES OF CASTELAZZO, *a portrait painter*

GIROLAMO PRIULI, *Doge of Venice*

MAID IN SHYLOCK'S HOUSE*

PATRICIANS AND OTHERS
(at director's discretion)

*Who should also be singer at end of play.

ACT ONE

Scene One

Venice, 1563. The Ghetto Nuovo. SHYLOCK's study. It is strewn with books and manuscripts.

SHYLOCK, a 'loan-banker', with his friend, ANTONIO, a merchant, are leisurely cataloguing.

ANTONIO is by the table, writing, as SHYLOCK reads out the titles and places them on his shelves.

They are old friends, and old: in their middle sixties.

SHYLOCK (*reading out*). 'Guide to the Perplexed'. Author, Maimonides, Ram-bam, known as the Great Eagle. Cairo. Twelfth century.

ANTONIO *writes.*

Hebrew/Hebrew Dictionary. Author, R. David Kimhi. England. Twelfth century. Not too fast for you, Antonio?

ANTONIO. It's not the most elegant script, but I'm speedy.

SHYLOCK. And I'm eager. I know it. But here, the last of the manuscripts and then we'll begin cataloguing my printed books. Such treasures to show you, you'll be thrilled, thrrrrrilled! You'll be — I can't wait . . . just one more —

ANTONIO. Do I complain?

SHYLOCK. — and then we'll rest. I promise you. I'll bring out my wines, and fuss and — the last one. I promise, promise.

ANTONIO. Shylock! Look! I'm waiting.

SHYLOCK. I have a saint for a friend.

ANTONIO. And what does the poor saint have?

SHYLOCK. An overgrown schoolboy. I know it! The worst of the deal. But —

ANTONIO. I'm waiting, Shylock.

SHYLOCK. Deed. Legal. Anglo-Jewish. Twelfth century. Author — I can't read the name. Probably drawn up by a businessman himself. (*Peering.*) What a mastery of Talmudic Law. I love them, those old men, their cleverness, their deeds, their wide-ranging talents. Feel it! Touch it!

ANTONIO. The past.

SHYLOCK. Exactly!

ANTONIO. And all past.

SHYLOCK. Antonio! You look sad.

ANTONIO. Sad?

SHYLOCK. I've overworked you. Here. Drink. Why should we wait till we're finished? (*Offers wine.*) Drink. It's a special day.

They drink in silence.

ANTONIO. So many books.

SHYLOCK. And all hidden for ten years. Do you know what that means for a collector? Ten years? Ha! The scheme of things! 'The Talmud and kindred Hebrew literature? Blasphemy!' they said, 'burn them!' And there they burned, on the Campo dei Fiori in Rome, decreed by Julius the Third of blessed origin, August the 12th, 1553, and followed swiftly by our very own and honoured Council of Ten in Venice. The day of the burning of the books. Except mine, which I hid, all of them, even my secular works. When fever strikes them you can't trust those warriors of God. With anything of learning? Never! That's what they really hated, not the books of the Jews but the books of men. I mean — MEN! Their spites, you see, the books revealed to them their thin minds. And do you think it's over even now? Look! (*Pushes out a secret section of his bookcase.*) The Sacred Books. The others I can bring back, but still, to this day, the Talmud is forbidden. And I have them, the greatest of them,

Bomberg's edition, each of them, starting 1519 to the last on June the 3rd, 1523. Aren't they beautiful?

ANTONIO. So beautiful.

SHYLOCK (*referring to others*). I've friends who buy for me all over the world. I'm a hoarder of other men's genius. My vice. My passion. Nothing I treasure more, except my daughter. So — drink! It's a special day. Look! A present to cheer you up. One of my most treasured manuscripts, a thirteenth-century book of precepts, author Isaac of Corbeil, with additamenta made by the students. I used to do it myself, study and scribble my thoughts in the margin. We all did it. We had keen minds, Antonio, very profound we thought ourselves, commenting on the meaning of life, the rights and wrongs of the laws, offering our interpretations of the interpretations of the great scholars who interpreted the meaning of the meaning of the prophets. 'Did the prophecies of Daniel refer to the historic events or to the Messianic times, or neither? Is the soul immortal, or not? Should one or should one not ride in a gondola on the Sabbath?' Money lending was never a full-time occupation and the Ghetto rocked with argument — ha! I love it! (*Pause.*) There! I *have* tired you.

ANTONIO. I assure you —

SHYLOCK. Depressed you, then. I've done that.

ANTONIO. Not that either. But —

SHYLOCK. But what? What but, then?

ANTONIO. Those books. Look at them. How they reminded me what I am, what I've done. Nothing! A merchant! A purchaser of this to sell there. A buyer up and seller off. And do you know, I hardly ever see my trade. I have an office, a room of ledgers and a table, and behind it I sit and wait till someone comes in to ask have I wool from Spain, cloth from England, cotton from Syria, wine from Crete. And I say yes, I've a ship due in a week, or a month, and I make a note, and someone goes to the dock, collects the corn, delivers it to an address, and I see nothing. I travel neither to England to check cloth, nor Syria to check cotton, or Corfu to see that the olive oil is cleanly corked, and I could steal time for myself in such places. It never worried me, this absence of curiosity for travel. Until I met you, old Jew —

SHYLOCK. Not so old *then,* old man, only just past fifty —

ANTONIO. — and I became caught up in your, your passion, your hoardings, your — your vices!

SHYLOCK. Is he complaining or thanking me?

ANTONIO. You've poisoned me, old Shylock, with restlessness and discontent, and at so late a time.

SHYLOCK. He's complaining.

ANTONIO. A lawyer, a doctor, a diplomat, a teacher — anything but a merchant. I'm so ashamed. There's no sweetness in my dealings. After the thrill of the first exchange, after the pride of paying a thousand ducats with one hand and taking fifteen hundred with the other — no skill. Just an office and some ledgers. It's such a joyless thing, a bargain. I'm so weary with trade.

Scene Two

SHYLOCK's *study. He and* ANTONIO *have been drinking.*

SHYLOCK. I gave you wine to cheer you up. It's cheered me down!

ANTONIO. The work's done. You should be happy! I've lost the use of my hand, but what of that? Look, order! Filed, catalogued, all that knowledge. You could save the world.

SHYLOCK. When I can't be certain of saving myself? What a thought! Not even the sages with all their wisdom could save themselves. Here, read this elegy on the Martyrs of Blois by the Rabbi Yom Tov of Joingy. What a lovely old man he must have been. To a question once about whether or not to use a stove on the Sabbath, he replied 'May my lot be with those who are warm, not those who are stringent!' Poor sage. They were all poor sages. Constantly invited to run educational establishments here and there, and never certain whether they were running into a massacre. From the

massacre of Rouen they fled into the massacre of London;
from the massacre of London into the massacre of York, and
from the massacre of York no one fled! (*Pause.*) Travelling
wasn't very safe in those days!

ANTONIO. Are you a religious man, Shylock?

SHYLOCK. What a question. Are you *so* drunk?

ANTONIO. You *are* religious, for all your freethinking, you're a
devout man. And I love and envy you for it.

SHYLOCK. You are *so* drunk. Religious! It's the condition of
being Jewish, like pimples with adolescence, who can help it?
Even those of us who don't believe in God have dark
suspicions that he believes in us. Listen, I'll tell you how it all
happened. Ha! The scheme of things! I love it! Imagine this
tribe of semites in the desert. Pagan, wild, but brilliant. A
sceptical race, believing only in themselves. Loving but
assertive. Full of quarrels and questions. Who could control
them? Leader after leader was thrown up but, in a tribe
where every father of his family was a leader, who could hold
them in check for long? Until one day a son called Abraham
was born, and he grew up knowing his brethren very, very
well indeed. 'I know how to control this arrogant, anarchic
herd of heathens,' he said to himself. And he taught them
about one God. Unseen! Of the spirit! That appealed to
them, the Hebrews, they had a weakness for concepts of the
abstract. An unseen God! Ha! I love it! What an inspiration.
But that wasn't all. Abraham's real statesmanship, his real
stroke of genius was to tell this tribe of exploding minds and
vain souls: 'Behold! An unseen God! God of the Universe! Of
all men! and —' wait, for here it comes, '— and, of all men
you are his chosen ones!' Irresistible! In an instant they were
quiet. Subdued. 'Oh! Oh! Chosen? Really? Us? To do what?'
'To bear witness to what is beautiful in creation, and just. A
service, not a privilege!' 'Oh dear! Chosen to bear witness!
What an honour! Ssh! Not so loud. Dignity! Abraham is
speaking. Respect! Listen to him. Order!' It worked! They
had God and Abraham had them. But — they were now
cursed. For from that day moved they into a nationhood
that had to be better than any other and, poor things, all

other nations found them unbearable to live with. What can I do? I'm chosen. I *must* be religious.

ANTONIO. I love you more and more, Shylock. You have a sanity I could not live without now. I'm spoiled, chosen also.

SHYLOCK. But sad, still. I can see it. I've failed to raise your spirits one tiny bit.

ANTONIO. *I'm* not a religious man. I had a letter today, from an old friend, Ansaldo Visconti of Milan, a rich merchant, and well-loved in my youth. But I'd forgotten him. And in this letter he talked of his misfortune, his downfall into ruin through strange and cursed events which I couldn't make any sense of, it was so wordy and maudlin and full of old times. And in the end he commends to me his only son, Bassanio, my godson it seems. And I'd forgotten him also. Poor young Bassanio. Probably a very noble young nobleman. I even think he must be a young patrician. His father was born in Venice, if I remember, of patrician stock, if I remember. No, he's probably a swaggering young braggart! Coming to see me in the hope I'll put trade his way, or put him in trade's way, or keep him by me as an assistant, passing on wisdom, or something. (*Pause.*) Here, Bassanio, a little piece of wisdom, here, in my pocket. (*Pause, mock pomp.*) I am now going to be wise! (*Pause. Then as if calling a dog.*) Here, wisdom, here, boy. Sit. Still. Quiet now. There, Bassanio, sits wisdom. (*Pause.*) I don't want to be wise, or to talk about trade, or to see him. Ungodly man! Doesn't that make me an ungodly man? I should never have had godsons. Not the type. Bachelor merchant. On the other hand I suppose that's just the type.

SHYLOCK. When do you expect him?

ANTONIO. Oh, tomorrow, or the next day, or is it next week? Can't remember which. Bassanio! Humph! (*Shouting out.*) I'm not a religious man, Bassanio.

SHYLOCK. Antonio, my friend, it's late. In ten minutes they lock the gates of the Ghetto and all good Christians should be outside.

ANTONIO (*still shouting*). I may be your godfather, Bassanio, but I'm not a religious man.

SHYLOCK. I have a suggestion.

ANTONIO. Bassanio, Bassanio!

SHYLOCK. Stay the night.

ANTONIO. Stay the night?

SHYLOCK. It's not permitted, but with money —

ANTONIO. What about Bassanio, in search of wisdom?

SHYLOCK. We'll send a message in the morning to say where you can be found. Stay. You know my house, lively, full of people in and out all the time. My daughter, Jessica, will look after you — if she deigns to talk that is.

ANTONIO. Very haughty, your Jessica.

SHYLOCK. And free and fractious but — cleverer than her illiterate old father. Gave her all the tutors I couldn't have. But soon I will have one of my own.

ANTONIO (*trumpeting*). Abtalion da Modena the illustrious!

SHYLOCK. My very own scholar.

ANTONIO. Arriving any day now, as he keeps assuring us.

SHYLOCK. Any day now.

ANTONIO (*still trumpeting*). On his very own pilgrimage from Lisbon to the holy Jerusalem, financed by his very own pupil here, Shylock Kolner, in return for his very own wisdom. (*As if calling a dog.*) Here, wisdom, here, boy!

SHYLOCK. Stay! You know how the Ghetto is constantly filled with visitors. In the morning Solomon Usque the writer is coming with the daughter from the Portuguese banking house of Mendes, and in the afternoon we'll go to the synagogue to hear the sermon of a very famous Rabbi from Florence, preaching on the importance of the Talmudic laws on cleanliness, with special reference to Aristotle! Stay. It'll be full of Venetian intelligentsia, they're always coming to attend the festivals, listen to the music. Very exotic we are. We fascinate them all, whether from England where they've expelled us, or Spain where they burn us. Stay. (*Pause.*) He's asleep. He'll have to stay. (*Taking the arm of the now half-asleep* ANTONIO, *he struggles with him towards a bedroom.*) And if the gatekeepers remember and come looking don't worry, I'll keep them happy. Happy, happy, happy.

Scene Three

SHYLOCK's *main room. Next morning. An atmosphere of great activity.* JESSICA, *helped by* SHYLOCK's *old sister,* RIVKA, *and a* MAID, *is supervising the comings and goings, in preparation for the midday meal.* TUBAL, *his partner, is going through accounts.*

JESSICA. We shall be six to eat at midday. Yesterday it was eight, the day before seven, and tomorrow, no doubt, more again. And is he up? He's not even awake yet. Eleven o'clock and he sleeps.

RIVKA. Yesterday was a very special day for him, Jessica. The books, remember, came out of hiding.

JESSICA. He dusted his dusty books! Heaven help me, Aunt Rivka, I have to look at those books again. From my earliest days I remember nothing but this madness, this illness for books. And at fifteen I thanked God that they had to be hidden away.

RIVKA. That's a sinful thing to say, niece. Your father would be ashamed to hear you talk like this.

JESSICA. My father is an intellectual snob. Every passing scholar or Rabbi, or eminent physician has to dine at his table. Some men fawn before crowns, he before degrees. And soon he'll have his very own scholar to come and stay and stay and stay and stay and —

RIVKA. When Abtalion Da Modena comes —

JESSICA. 'When Abtalion Da Modena comes! Wait till Abtalion Da Modena comes!' My father promises him as some men promise the Messiah!

RIVKA. This is not worthy of you, Jessica. Scholarship must be respected.

JESSICA. Oh, I respect scholarship, but there is a world outside
the covers of a book, isn't there? Men don't always behave as
the philosophers fear, do they? I have the sayings and
warnings of sages ringing in my ears so loudly, that music,
which I adore above all things, can hardly make sense in my
head any more.

TUBAL. Your father is a special man, Jessica. He's animated by
ideas. 'Keep me moving,' he cries, 'don't let the dark
overtake me, it's my only hope.' A man not afraid to have his
mind changed? That's rare. I wish I had such courage.

JESSICA. But he bullies with it all, Uncle Tubal. My father's
cruelty is to diminish whoever can't recall a name, a date, an
event, or argument. Patterns! The world's fortunes move in
patterns. 'The scheme of things.' Well, I do not believe there
is a scheme of things, only chaos and misery, and —

RIVKA. That's wanton!

JESSICA. — and in it we must carve out just sufficient order for
an ounce of happiness.

RIVKA. Wanton!

JESSICA. Nothing too ambitious. A little modest sweetness, at
any price.

RIVKA. At any price?

JESSICA. At almost any price. We have no choice. There are
madmen at large in the world. All writing books! Men fired
by this ideal, that passion, full of dogma about the way other
men should live, assuming moralities for us, deciding the
limits of our pleasure, our endeavour, our abilities, our pain.
Decreed by whom? By what right? My father is full of them
and I am oppressed by them and I think my time is done for
them. (*She leaves.*)

RIVKA. She exaggerates. My brother's not a tyrannical father.

TUBAL. Of course not. When their quarrels are over, Shylock
makes light of it. But I fear he confuses her frustrations for
her originality.

RIVKA. He wanted to prove that daughters could achieve the

intellectual stature of sons.

TUBAL. A wilful thought I've always thought. But there you are, you can't discuss children with parents, you offend them where they've placed their most cherished endeavour.

A young man, RODERIGUES DA CUNHA, *rushes in. He carries rolls of plans.*

RODERIGUES. Shylock! Shylock! The plans of the new synagogue! No Shylock?

RIVKA. Asleep still.

RODERIGUES. Asleep still. My appointment was for eleven.

TUBAL. As was mine. 'The accounts,' he cries, 'the accounts are in disorder.'

RODERIGUES. 'The plans,' he cries, 'the plans! You want me to contribute to the building of a new synagogue? Let me see the plans first.' So I stay up all night to draw a new set of plans, and he sleeps!

RIVKA. Go into the kitchen, Roderigues, Jessica is there.

RODERIGUES. All night!

RIVKA. Calm yourself —

RODERIGUES. Well, not *all* night.

RIVKA. — take mid-morning refreshment but don't complain to her, she's a little — heavy. My brother will be with us soon.

RODERIGUES *nearly succeeds in leaving but is forced back into the room by a storming* JESSICA.

JESSICA. Did you know they were coming *now?*

RIVKA. Who, my dear, who?

JESSICA. Solomon Usque and Rebecca da Mendes.

TUBAL. But these are honours, Jessica.

JESSICA. Honours for you, work for me, and overcrowding for the Ghetto. Suddenly Venice is alive with Portuguese Anusim.

RIVKA. Fleeing the Inquisition, child, what are you saying?

JESSICA. They will be welcome, but I'm not told, I'm not told.

Enter SOLOMON USQUE *and* REBECCA DA MENDES.

USQUE. Solomon Usque, playwright of Lisbon, otherwise known as Duarte de Pinel. May I present the Signora Rebecca da Mendes, daughter of the late Francisco Mendes, banker of Lisbon. Peace be unto you, Signor Shylock.

TUBAL. You're both known and welcome, but I'm not Shylock. Tubal di Ponti, his friend and partner, and honoured.

REBECCA. He's always greeting the wrong person —

USQUE. — pushing the wrong door —

REBECCA. — drinking from the wrong shaped glass!

USQUE. When artists aspire to elegance they end by being ridiculous. Please, when will friend Shylock appear?

SHYLOCK *enters accompanied by* ANTONIO.

SHYLOCK. He appears, he appears! Friend Shylock appears! Signora Mendes, Signor Usque, I'm ashamed to have had no one waiting for you at the door. May I present my daughter Jessica; my sister Rivka; my good friend Antonio Querini, a merchant of Venice whose head is not his own this morning, and my partner, Tubal di Ponti. Oh yes, and Roderigues — er —

RODERIGUES. — da Cunha.

SHYLOCK. — da Cunha, architect. They're building a new synagogue, to be situated on the south side of the Campiello delle Scuole. Of all people you must know of the plans. Your father, Signora, renowned! Renowned!

REBECCA. There are so many —

SHYLOCK. No, no! We are all indebted. No comparison: benevolence! statesmanship! Whatever I can do for you will be nothing in return. Nothing.

JESSICA. I must attend to the food. Please excuse me.

RODERIGUES. I will join you. Forgive me, everyone, I'm dying of thirst.

SHYLOCK. Thirst! My goodness. Look at me! Jessica, the citronade.

JESSICA (*leaving*). It's on the table, father.

SHYLOCK. Soon, dear Roderigues, I'll be with you soon.

RODERIGUES (*leaving*). Beautiful! Beautiful plans!

> *They go.* SHYLOCK *pours drinks which he gives to* RIVKA *to hand out.*

SHYLOCK. Everything is beautiful to him.

RIVKA. Especially my niece.

SHYLOCK. But not he to her! Stop match-making! He's a sweet boy but not her match. She always match-makes. And always the wrong one. She'll marry the wrong man without your help, push not! (*To his guests.*) Now, what news do you bring?

USQUE. The news is not 'beautiful' either.

SHYLOCK. Tell us.

USQUE. What point in the details, their awfulness is monotonous.

REBECCA. We need help, let's talk about that.

SHYLOCK. Tell us.

USQUE. In the last year the Coimbra Tribunal, which has jurisdiction over the Northern provinces of Portugal, has held thirty-five autos-da-fé drawn from different towns and villages of Traz-os-Montes and Beira alone.

REBECCA. In addition to which the Lisbon and Evora Tribunals have tried Anusim arrested in towns situated in the Eastern department of Braganza.

USQUE. Fifty people burnt at the stake.

REBECCA. Old women, young men, relatives, friends.

USQUE. Marian Fernandes, a cousin from Lisbon.

REBECCA. Maria Diez, my old aunt from Guarda.

USQUE. Sebastian Rodrigo Pinto, a friend from Lamego.

REBECCA. Diego Della Rogna, his wife Isabelle Nones, their four daughters and two sons.

USQUE. An entire family burnt.

REBECCA. Facing each other.

Silence.

But there are survivors. It's to those we must attend. Signor Shylock, we are among friends?

SHYLOCK. Everyone, inseparable.

REBECCA. I have been told that you are a courageous man —

SHYLOCK. Please! A fool with my chances, perhaps —

REBECCA. During the next months, a steady stream of the Portuguese community will be making their way to Ancona before leaving for Salonika. Though not easy, Venice is the least dangerous place for them to stop en route and rest. We would like you to arrange places for them to stay, families who would put them up, and a fund started to assist their journey.

RIVKA. And who else but my brother!

SHYLOCK. Who else! I'd have been offended had anyone else been approached. You knew who to come to, didn't you?

REBECCA. We'd been told.

SHYLOCK. They talk, you see, Antonio! I'm a name in my community. From nobody to somebody, a name! Now, you'll stay for food, you must eat with us.

RIVKA. Of course they'll stay and eat with us. You imagine I wouldn't ask them to stay and eat.

SHYLOCK. Say you'll stay, please, please, I insist.

RIVKA. We all insist.

SHYLOCK. We all insist. And you must allow me to show you my collection of manuscripts, come.

USQUE. Signora Mendes is the collector, I only write them.

SHYLOCK. You must persuade him to sign one of his books for me.

USQUE. Ha! they hardly perform me let alone print me.

REBECCA. Fortunately he has other skills.

USQUE. Self-appointed plenipotentiary for refugees.

REBECCA. A constant occupation but one giving him great opportunity for travel — from Constantinople to London.

SHYLOCK. To London?

RIVKA. Are there still Jews in England?

REBECCA. Hardly any. A clandestine existence. But we go back and forth for trade.

SHYLOCK. Then you must look out for a rare manuscript for me — The Fox's Fables.

REBECCA. What's your special interest?

SHYLOCK. There's an edition in the library of Exeter Cathedral written by the author *himself* in which he complains about his life in England and the indifference of its wealthy Jews to intellectual and literary activities.

USQUE. Perhaps *that* accounts for the massacre of London.

SHYLOCK, REBECCA *and* RIVKA *prepare to leave.*

REBECCA (*to* SHYLOCK *as they're leaving*). I shall never understand this habit of using our misery to feed our wit.

USQUE (*parting shot as they go off*). What else is left to feed it, Signora?

SHYLOCK. And the plans for the synagogue! We simply must look at the plans for the new Spanish synagogue together.

Exit with REBECCA *and* RIVKA.

USQUE. Is that how it is every day?

TUBAL. Every day! Brother and sister rivalling one another in hospitality, and daughter pushing the other way. A house never still.

ANTONIO. When he's not negotiating loans, he's dispatching men around the world to buy him books, or opening the sights of the Ghetto to visiting dignitaries. Wait till his very own scholar arrives, there'll be time for nothing but tutorials and debate. The very air will be thick with 'wisdom'. So he thinks.

TUBAL. Though in time you'll find he's a very melancholy man, will you agree, Signor Antonio?

ANTONIO. In my warehouse is a young man, Graziano Sanudo, in charge of the import of spices. Now *he's* a happy man, no melancholy in him, and I don't know that I can stand him around. He has no real opinions, simply bends with the wind, quickly rushing to agree with the next speaker. He's a survivor, not defiantly, which is honourable, but creepily, like a chameleon, blending with everyone to avoid anyone's sting. He laughs when every idiot farts out thin wit, fawns on the tyrannical, is reverential before the papal, and manifests the most depressingly boisterous happiness I know. Give me Shylock's melancholy, gentlemen, and take away my man's smiles.

TUBAL. But Jessica is right. Shylock's kind of intelligence *is* an illness.

ANTONIO. Aye! You die from it in the end.

USQUE. I see he has an eternal friend in you, Signor Antonio.

ANTONIO. And I in him. Now, gentlemen, excuse me. I've been expecting a young man to call for me here in search of wisdom, and I fear he's lost.

TUBAL. The message went to your offices, Antonio, first thing this morning. Come at once to the Ghetto Nuovo between the German Synagogue and the Association for the Jewish Poor. Ground floor, ask if lost.

ANTONIO. Thank you, but I've no knowing what kind of soul he is, simple or bright. And in case the former, I'd better go out in search. I think I need the air, besides. (*Leaves.*)

USQUE. Your community lives well, I see. You can build your synagogues and depend upon gentile friends.

TUBAL. Personally I depend upon no gentile but, misery is difficult to wear all weathers. We survive from contract to contract, not knowing if after five years it will be renewed, and if renewed whether it will be for another five, or ten or three but —

USQUE. — Trade is trade —

TUBAL. — Trade is trade and they know it also, and we pay! An annual tribute of twenty thousand ducats; another twenty thousand for renting these squalid walls; fifteen thousand more to the Navy Board — for God knows what; another hundred for the upkeep of the canals, which stink! And, on top of all that, ten thousand more in time of war which, since our beloved and righteous republic seems constantly fighting with someone or other ensures that sum too as a regular payment. Why, sometimes there's barely pennies in the Ghetto. For days we're all borrowing off each other, till new funds flow in. Only fourteen hundred souls, remember. We're no more than that, trapped in an oppressive circus with three water wells and a proclivity for fires.

SHYLOCK *enters*.

SHYLOCK (*calling*). Roderigues! In here! Bring the plans in here, the light's better.

RODERIGUES *struggles in with rolls of plans*.

Signor Usque, *you* must look at these plans for the Spanish synagogue. (*To* RODERIGUES.) Now, the entrance, why so plain? Why no wrought iron gates? They're Spanish, come from a highly cultured background!

ANTONIO *and* BASSANIO *enter at this point but hold back to watch and listen*.

TUBAL (*continuing to* USQUE). And I make no mention of special demands in times of 'special distress', nor of the unreturned 'loans' to the treasury which bring in no more than a four per cent rate of interest. And did I leave out the cost of upkeeping our own community services and our own streets? I did, I did!

RODERIGUES. And did you leave out the bribes demanded by petty officials?

TUBAL. I did! I did!

RODERIGUES. And payments to the local church? the local police?

SHYLOCK. He did! He did! But never mind about politics. Why is the facade so dull? Is the new mint dull? Or the library and museum of antiquities? And the windows! There's no light!

RODERIGUES. Give me the taxes of Venice and I'll give you light!

SHYLOCK. You don't need money to be bold. You need boldness! Take them away and think again. Bolder! Be bolder!

ANTONIO (*finally making himself known*). Gentlemen, allow me to introduce my godson, Bassanio Visconti.

SHYLOCK. Ah, Antonio. You found him. Welcome, young man, welcome. You'll stay to eat with us, won't you? Do you know anything about architecture? We're building a new synagogue, look. We don't have a Palladio to build us a San Giorgio Maggiore, but with our modest funds . . .

ANTONIO. I don't think Bassanio plans to stay, but we would like to talk together, and if —

SHYLOCK. But of course, Friend Roderigues is leaving.

RODERIGUES. To be bolder!

TUBAL. And I have sights to show Signor Usque.

SHYLOCK. The first time godfather and son meet is a special and private time. (*To* TUBAL *as he and* SHYLOCK *prepare to leave.*) Tubal, you *should* look at these plans for the new synagogue before they're folded away. It's your money too, you know.

TUBAL. I'm plan blind, Shylock. They mean nothing to me. *You* spend my money.

They leave.

BASSANIO. And that is a Jew?

ANTONIO (*reprimanding*). *He* is a Jew.

BASSANIO. I don't think I know what to say.

ANTONIO. Have you never met one before?

BASSANIO. Talked of, described, imagined, but —

ANTONIO. Shylock is my special friend.

BASSANIO. Then, sir, he must be a special man.

ANTONIO (*suspicious and changing the subject*). Your father speaks highly of you and begs me to help where I can.

BASSANIO. My lord Antonio —

ANTONIO. I'm not a lord, I'm a patrician — lapsed and indifferent to their politicking but, a patrician nonetheless.

BASSANIO. Lord, patrician — you are my godfather.

ANTONIO. I'd forgotten.

BASSANIO. Oh, understandably, understandably! The early years were so full of my father's talk of you and your goodness and your good time together, but — he made no effort to make us known to one another. It was a cause of distress between us.

ANTONIO. There were good times together, were there?

BASSANIO. He spoke of little else. What he shared with you, I shared. What happened between you, I saw happen. If I did wrong he'd say, your godfather would not approve of that. And as I grew I did what I did, thought what I thought, saying to myself — what would the good Antonio do now, how would the wise Antonio decide?

ANTONIO. Ah, wisdom! I feared it.

BASSANIO. You must surely have experienced this yourself, sir, that in your mind there is always one person, a vivid critic, whose tone of voice and special use of words is there in your brain, constantly.

ANTONIO. They call him God, Bassanio.

BASSANIO. I think you're mocking me. Have I come at a wrong time? Perhaps I shouldn't have come at all. To be honest, I hate arriving behind letters of recommendation, it's so undignified and besides, what can the poor host do but be courteous, obliging. Forgive me, sir. You know nothing of me. I'll go. But I'll find ways of making myself

ACT ONE SCENE THREE 19

known to you, and useful, and in the coming months I'll
try to earn your trust. Goodbye, sir.

ANTONIO. No, no, no. Don't go, young man. I've been rude
and discourteous, forgive me. Bachelors have special dreads.
Old age, loneliness, too much noise, too many requests; we
fear opportunists and women. Senile fears. Forgive me. Sit
and talk about yourself and what you want of me. Of course
I remember your father. We were good for one another in
lean years. Talk. I'll help his son. Without question. Trade?
Tricks of the trade? Contracts? To represent me? Tell me
what you want.

BASSANIO. In Belmont, sir, there is a lady.

ANTONIO. Ah, love!

BASSANIO. Her father's family goes back to the time when
Venetians were fishermen, and —

ANTONIO. And would now prefer to forget it!

BASSANIO. — And, like all of those ancient families, became
wealthy. These, the Contarinis, added to their wealth with —
what shall I call it? — not madness, but — unorthodoxy. The
father of my lady, whose name is Portia, was — well — odd!
A philosopher.

ANTONIO. Oh, very odd.

BASSANIO. He evolved, it seems, a strange theory that men's
character could be learned by tests, and to this end he
devised a huge chart divided into the most important aspects
of a man's character. Honour, common sense, loyalty,
stamina and so on. And for each virtue and its opposite he
devised their tests. His entire estates became manned by men
he'd chosen based upon these philosophically evolved
examinations. All, with one exception, fell into ruin.

ANTONIO. What an incredibly sad story.

BASSANIO. There is a happy side. The daughter —

ANTONIO. Beautiful?

BASSANIO. Well, not beautiful perhaps, but — striking, vivid.
Compelling. Intelligent eyes, mobile features — handsome. In

fact, if I must be blunt, determination and strength of will give her face a masculine aspect. She's feminine to the extent that she doesn't deny her sex, yet misleading because she doesn't cultivate, exploit, abuse it.

ANTONIO. Just such a woman I'd like to have met in *my* youth.

BASSANIO. You'll understand, then, the reason for my agitation.

ANTONIO. But not yet how it concerns me.

BASSANIO. Three caskets rest at Belmont. One gold, one silver, one lead. Who chooses the correct casket wins the daughter.

ANTONIO. Aha! The final test. And my role in this?

BASSANIO. I've lived a stupid, wasting life, Signor Antonio. I possess nothing and can lay my hands on nothing. I had hoped to marry wealth but now I've fallen in love with ruins. I mean to choose the right casket, marry that extraordinary woman and work to restore her property to profit. But I'm without means either to dress myself or reach her.

ANTONIO. It will cost?

BASSANIO. To present myself without insult? Three thousand ducats.

ANTONIO. Three thousand ducats!

BASSANIO. I believe no claim was ever made on your godfathership before.

ANTONIO. None.

BASSANIO. And none will be again.

ANTONIO. Bassanio, you come at a bad time. I've ships to sea but no cash to hand. More, I plan retirement, and all my wealth lies in their cargoes. The small change I need for daily living is easily got on credit from friendly traders, but the eyes of the Rialto are on me and I know no one who'll lend me so large a sum except —

BASSANIO. Who?

ANTONIO. Shylock.

BASSANIO. The Jew?

ANTONIO (*defying his contempt*). Shylock.

BASSANIO. But the interest rate, the conditions.

ANTONIO. Whatever the conditions! It's more than I've ever borrowed in my life, but for the good years of my youth with your father, done!

BASSANIO. With a Jew!

ANTONIO. I've told you, young man, the Jew is my special friend.

BASSANIO. Of course. Forgive me, sir. And now, I'll go. If there's anything I can do for you in the city?

ANTONIO. Yes, take a message to my assistant, Graziano Sanudo. Tell him I won't be in today, but to arrange for dinner on Wednesday. I'm entertaining my friend, Shylock, so no pork. Join us, Bassanio, I keep a good wine cellar.

BASSANIO. With the greatest of pleasure, and honoured. May I bring with me an old friend I've recently met again? A sort of philosopher.

ANTONIO. 'Sort of'?

BASSANIO. Writes poetry occasionally.

ANTONIO. A 'sort of philosopher' who 'writes poetry occasionally!' Good! Old Shylock might enjoy that. What's his name?

BASSANIO. Lorenzo Pisani.

ANTONIO. Ah! The silk manufacturers.

BASSANIO. You know them?

ANTONIO. The fabric, not the family.

BASSANIO. You won't regret this trust, Signor.

ANTONIO. I hope to God I do not, Bassanio.

BASSANIO *leaving, meets* SHYLOCK *on the way out.* SHYLOCK *bows but is ignored.*

I hope to God.

SHYLOCK. And what was that like?

ANTONIO. I'm not certain. He'd not met a Jew before.

SHYLOCK *goes into fits of laughter.*

ANTONIO. What is so funny?

SHYLOCK That's not a sin. There are a hundred million people in China who've not met a Jew before!

ANTONIO. Still he worries me for other reasons. There was too much calculation in him. You'll be meeting him on Wednesday and can judge for yourself. I've invited him for dinner. With a friend of his, Lorenzo Pisani.

SHYLOCK. Pisani?

ANTONIO. You know him?

SHYLOCK. I know him. He wrote a poem once, too long, 'The Ruin of the Nation's Heart'. A murky thing, full of other people's philosophy. Jessica showed it to me. She seemed very impressed because it called for a return to simplicity . . .

ANTONIO. Of course! My assistant Graziano showed it *me.* Seems it set our youth on fire, full of disgust with the great wretchedness of the world and the sins of men. It had a sense of doom which the poet seemed to enjoy rather more than he was anxious to warn of.

SHYLOCK. That's the one! Ah, children, children! (*Which reminds him, so he calls.*) Children! Children! Let's eat. (*To* ANTONIO.) You must be starving, and the Portuguese must be bored to death with my books by now, and we must be finished eating in time for a sitting. (*Calling again.*) Jessica. (*To* ANTONIO.) I'm having our portrait painted. It's the day for a sitting. A great painter, an old man now, but exquisite, Moses of Castelazzo. Renowned!

ANTONIO. Shylock?

SHYLOCK. My friend!

ANTONIO. I have a great favour to ask of you.

SHYLOCK. At last! A favour! Antonio of Shylock!

ANTONIO. To borrow three thousand ducats.

SHYLOCK. Not four? Five? Ten?

ANTONIO. I'm not making jokes, Shylock.

SHYLOCK. And why do you think I make jokes?

ANTONIO. For three months?

SHYLOCK. Your city borrows forever, why not three months for you?

ANTONIO. You know my position?

SHYLOCK. I know your position. Your fortune in one voyage, I know. Insane. Still.

ANTONIO. You're a good man, old man.

SHYLOCK. Old man — forever! Good — not always. I'm a friend.

ANTONIO. What shall you want as a surety in the contract?

SHYLOCK. The *what*?

ANTONIO. The contract, Shylock. We must draw up a bond.

SHYLOCK. A bond? Between friends? What nonsense are you talking, Antonio?

ANTONIO. The law demands it.

SHYLOCK. Then we'll ignore the law.

ANTONIO. The law demands: no dealings may be made with Jews unless covered by a legal bond.

SHYLOCK. That law was made for enemies, not friends.

ANTONIO. I don't want it for myself, Shylock, but for you. If word gets out we've made no bond then, *you'll* be penalised, not I.

SHYLOCK. And who will tell?

ANTONIO. It's known already. The money is not for me. My godson. No, don't tell me I'm a fool. The boy's father was a good friend. I told him you were the only man I know could raise that sum at once.

SHYLOCK. Good! Then lie to him.

ANTONIO. Shylock! The law says, in these very words, 'It is

forbidden to enter into dealings with a Jew without sign and
sealing of a bond, which bond must name the sums
borrowed, specify the collateral, name the day, the hour to
be paid, and —

TOGETHER. — and be witnessed by three Venetians, two
patricians and one citizen, and *then* registered!

ANTONIO. Be sensible! The law of Venice is a jealous one, no
man may bend it. The city's reputation *rests* on respect for
its laws.

SHYLOCK. Sensible! Sensible! I follow my heart, *my* laws.
What could be more sensible? The Deuteronic Code says
'Thou shalt not lend upon usury to thy brother. Unto a
foreigner thou mayest lend upon usury, but unto thy brother
not.' Your papacy, however, turns your laws against us. But
for once, Antonio, let us not quite bend the law but interpret
it as men, neither Christian nor Jew. I love you, therefore
you are my brother. And since you are my brother, my laws
say I may not lend upon usury to you, but must uphold you.
Take the ducats.

ANTONIO. But the laws of Venice are something else, dear
Shylock, dear brother. More important even than its
constitution.

SHYLOCK. The laws must leave me to conduct my loves as I
please.

ANTONIO. Especially now when the economy is so vulnerable.

SHYLOCK. My dealings with you are sacrosanct.

ANTONIO. The French markets are gone, the English are
building faster and better ships and there are fools talking
about dangerous protectionist policies. We are a nervous
Empire.

SHYLOCK. My heart needs to know I can trust and be trusted.

ANTONIO. You must not, cannot, bend the law.

SHYLOCK (*angry, with the law*). You can have three thousand
ducats but there will be no bond, for no collateral, and for no
time limit whatsoever.

ANTONIO. I understand. And it brings me closer to you than ever. But the deeper I feel our friendship the more compelled I feel to press my point, and protect you. You are a Jew, Shylock. Not only is your race a minority, it is despised. Your existence here in Venice, your pleasures, your very freedom to be sardonic or bitter is a privilege, not a right. Your life, the lives of your people depend upon contract and *your* respect for the laws behind contract, just as your contract with the city councillors *they* must respect. Therefore you, of all people, have need of that respect for the law. The law, Shylock, the law! For you and your people, the bond-in-law must be honoured.

SHYLOCK. Oh, you have really brought me down. That's earth I feel now. Solid. (*Pause, not losing his good humour.*) We'll cheat them yet.

ANTONIO. You mean you're still not persuaded?

SHYLOCK. I'm persuaded, oh yes, I'm very, very persuaded. We'll have a bond.

ANTONIO. Good!

SHYLOCK. A nonsense bond.

ANTONIO. A nonsense bond?

SHYLOCK. A lovely, loving nonsense bond. To mock the law.

ANTONIO. To mock?

SHYLOCK. Barbaric laws? Barbaric bonds! Three thousand ducats against a pound your flesh.

ANTONIO. My flesh?

SHYLOCK. You're like an idiot child suddenly. (*Mocking.*) 'A nonsense bond? My flesh?' Yes. If I am not repaid by you, upon the day, the hour, I'll have a pound of your old flesh, Antonio, from near that part of your body which pleases me most — your heart. Your heart, dearheart, and I'd take that, too, if I could, I'm so fond of it.

Pause as SHYLOCK *waits to see if* ANTONIO *accepts.*

ANTONIO. Barbaric laws, barbaric bonds?

SHYLOCK. Madness for the mad.

ANTONIO. Idiocies for the idiots.

SHYLOCK. Contempt for the contemptible.

ANTONIO. They mock our friendship —

SHYLOCK. — We mock their laws.

ANTONIO (*pinching himself*). Do I have a pound of flesh? I don't even have a pound of flesh.

SHYLCOK (*pinching him*). Here, and here, and here, one, two, three pounds of flesh!

He's tickling him; ANTONIO responds. Like children they're goosing each other and giggling, upon which note JESSICA and RIVKA enter with food, RODERIGUES also.

TUBAL, REBECCA and USQUE enter deep in animated conversation. A meal is to be eaten, the sounds and pleasures of hospitality are in the air.

Scene Four

ANTONIO's *warehouse. Bales of coloured cloth, some from* PISANI *factories. Sacks of spices.*

GRAZIANO, *throwing cloth over* BASSANIO *to see which suits him. He tends to have conversations with himself, ignoring what others are saying.*

LORENZO, *plunging his hand in a sack drawing spice pebbles which run back through his fingers.*

BASSANIO. I was amazed. 'And that is a Jew?' I asked. '*He* is a Jew,' my godfather corrected.

LORENZO. I don't like it. A world turned upside down.

BASSANIO. They were all Jews! His friends!

GRAZIANO. But a loan of three thousand ducats? I don't like it!

BASSANIO. You should have heard them, discussing Venice as though the city cared for their voice, existed for their judgement!

LORENZO. Money is a dead thing, with no seed, it's not fit to engender.

GRAZIANO. Well said.

BASSANIO. What could I do, Lorenzo? 'The Jew is my special friend,' he said.

GRAZIANO. Ah, now that *is* understandable.

LORENZO. Is it?

GRAZIANO. Well —

LORENZO. Shylock dares play God with a dead thing, and Venice has only a dead language to answer him with. Of course his usury flourishes. A nation that confuses timidity for tolerance is a nation without principle.

GRAZIANO. A nation turned upside down.

BASSANIO (*to* LORENZO). Do you know Shylock well?

LORENZO (*moving from sack to sack, the spices trickling through his hands*). I know him.

GRAZIANO (*Pursuing his own conversation with* BASSANIO *while winding cloth round him*). Who do you know asserts authority?

LORENZO. A loud, enthusiastic man.

GRAZIANO. Men fear earning hatreds! No leadership! No God!

LORENZO. I've stood by him in the Ghetto when he's showing visitors its sights.

GRAZIANO. Not even the priests have time for God and our painters paint their Virgin Marys like whores.

LORENZO. Thin achievements in stone which he's magnified more from relief they've any stones at all than from their real worth.

GRAZIANO. The aged are in control of Venice, my friends.

LORENZO. There's hysteria in his description of things. His tone is urgent —

GRAZIANO. A burning issue.

LORENZO. — excited —

GRAZIANO. I burn whenever it comes up.

LORENZO. — excited, ornate and proudly erudite.

GRAZIANO. It comes up burning and I burn.

LORENZO. That's his sin: intellectual pride. His daughter can't bear it.

BASSANIO. You know Shylock's daughter?

GRAZIANO. A friend of yours?

LORENZO. You'd not think they're of the same blood. He's proud, she's modest. He imagines knowledge is all, she lives in the world. His voice is metallic with contempt, hers is sweet with reason. And she listens to music.

BASSANIO. And poetry perhaps?

LORENZO. And poetry, perhaps.

BASSANIO. Even praised some?

LORENZO. Even that.

BASSANIO. Good God, Lorenzo, are you in love?

LORENZO. Love? Who knows about love? She admired the poem and those who admire us must have merit we think. Can that be love? Respect perhaps.

BASSANIO. What an uncertain young man! Is this the 'he' who wrote 'The Ruins of the Nation's Heart'?

LORENZO. You're right! My nature can't decide itself. I feel passionate appetites within me but for what? The fool depresses me yet I myself believe in God enough to risk being called a simpleton. I despise power yet so much offends me that I want power to wipe out the offence. And where does it lie? In trade or moral principle? The spirit of the trader is in me as in every Venetian but there is such a frenzy of avarice and unbridled ambition that I feel the end of the world must be near, a world which one moment I want to renounce, the next help save from itself.

BASSANIO. Beware, young man, beware. Help the poor world

save itself? Would you preach like Savanarola? He also
thought Italy lived in horrible times, look how he ended his
mission. The trap is that preachers intoxicate themselves so,
come to deem themselves lords of life and earth, abuse their
powers and weary men by perpetual admonitions. Beware,
young man, beware.

GRAZIANO. Beware, nothing! Lorenzo's right. Horrible times.
There's little for young men of character here.

BASSANIO. Nonsense! Everywhere I turn I hear of young
patricians being schooled for trade, diplomacy, the council's
work.

LORENZO. But can those young patricians vote for the doge if
they're under thirty, or become senators before forty? Power
doesn't reside in principle but in the hands of a few families.

BASSANIO. Who trade with the world! Come, what are you
saying? Venice is a free city. Her doors are open, open!

LORENZO. Her legs are open, open! Venice — brothel of the
Mediterranean. And all so that we can boast to everyone of
our local codes and a freedom which tolerates corruption.

BASSANIO. Steady there, Lorenzo. Not too far. The tolerance
of Jews may be unpalatable to us, but trade, I sometimes
think that men in trade have kept our mad world sane,
preserved us from destructive politicians. Venice built its
glory on its ancient trading families, after all.

GRAZIANO. And that's where the power lies, in the long
ancient families who trade. I should know, coming as I do
from one of them.

BASSANIO. *Long* ancient families? You?

GRAZIANO. Don't be surprised, my friends, not all Venetian
aristocracy is bright, you see. Least of all I. Me. Least of all
me. Or is it 'I'? I'm what they call an academic failure,
expect nothing of me. My family are wealthy but not
illustrious. They hoped I'd rise to be a statesman and add
honour to their fortune, but I've neither tact nor memory,
and in shame my family apprenticed me to trade. Personal
assistant and happy!

BASSANIO. But what is a 'long family'?

GRAZIANO. A long family it is us, jealously listed in the chronicles and lists of our nobility as one of the twenty-four families. Of old. Who began it all. Or rather, there are twelve, from which I come, who claim the greatest nobility because they go back before 762, or is it 726? When the first doge was elected, whose name was Orso, a military man, or was that Anafesto? Because some say the first doge was elected in 679, or was it 697? And that *his* name was Anafesto, or was *his* name Orso? Whoever, my family goes back beyond then. The other twelve families only claim to have elected him. But both are long families. So called. As you see.

BASSANIO. And all were fishermen?

GRAZIANO. No! I mean, yes! I mean, the point is, we don't think of ourselves as descended from fishermen. It's just that we're — old. Go back a long way. The Roman Empire. Venice as a second Rome. Ancient.

BASSANIO. To be ancient is to be noble, you mean?

GRAZIANO. Exactly what I'm trying to say.

BASSANIO. So, a peasant family if it had the memory and evidence of a long past would be noble too?

GRAZIANO. Ah, no.

BASSANIO. So that's *not* exactly what you're trying to say?

GRAZIANO. That's what I'm saying, not exactly.

BASSANIO. Something more is needed to be a noble family?

GRAZIANO. Power!

BASSANIO. Which comes from where?

GRAZIANO. Stop teasing me, Bassanio. The question of Venetian nobility is an anxious one, my family quibble about it constantly.

LORENZO. And pointlessly. The question remains. What's to become of Venice? Does strength lie in trade or moral principle?

BASSANIO. Now you talk of strength. I thought we were

talking of power.

LORENZO. You're right. We must distinguish our words or the concepts behind them will become entangled also.

BASSANIO. And strength may lie in moral principle but power resides in trade. See this pebble of pepper — it's this has the power to push men across seas. Three million pounds passed through Venice this year. Do you know what amount of gold that represents? Kings monopolise the spice trade for themselves.

LORENZO. But religious principle is constant, trade is not. A Portuguese sailor circumnavigates the Cape? The spice trade of the Mediterranean dies!

BASSANIO. And who takes over? The Portuguese! Another Catholic nation! And where is religious principle then?

LORENZO. More reason to defend it! For it would then have power to bind the trade of nations who would otherwise fight.

BASSANIO. Precisely! As I said! Trade keeps the world sane while the wild men rant on about their principles. Beware, young man, beware! Gentlemen, it's my time to go. I must cut my suits and sharpen my wits for Belmont. I chase a woman there they say has intellect.

LORENZO. And what is *her* inheritance? Ruins!

BASSANIO. Which she will rebuild.

LORENZO. If the elders will allow her.

BASSANIO. Despite them she will.

LORENZO. If their laws don't cripple her.

BASSANIO. I know her. She will.

LORENZO. If she has cunning and connections and the facility to fawn.

BASSANIO. She will, she will! Rebuild! As youth does, ignoring the evil within, defying the past. With my help of course. We're young! Don't be so solemn, Lorenzo. We'll meet at Antonio's for dinner and talk more. Perhaps we'll get to know you better, Graziano.

GRAZIANO. You'll love me, I promise you.

BASSANIO. And old Shylock too. What more will he be made of, I wonder?

LORENZO. Nothing much for loving there.

GRAZIANO. I know what he means, I know what he means.

Scene Five

SHYLOCK's *main room.*
Chairs and easel are being set up for a portrait sitting.
SHYLOCK *enters with* USQUE, *followed by a bustling* RIVKA, *and* RODERIGUES *who is planning to do his own sketch of* JESSICA.
The old Jewish portrait painter MOSES OF CASTELAZZO *arrives.*

SHYLOCK. Ah! Moses, you're here!

MOSES. No! I'm not here!

SHYLOCK. Signor Usque, playwright, allow me to introduce you to the painter, the renowned Moses of Castelazzo.

MOSES (*ignoring the niceties of introduction and going straight to the easel*). Renowned! Renowned! Who cares about renown at eighty!

SHYLOCK *and* RIVKA *take up positions.*

RODERIGUES. And where's Jessica? How can I draw a subject who's not there?

MOSES (*mocking*). And where's Jessica? How can I draw a subject who's not there! Look at him! If you must be in love don't show it. If you must show it don't draw it! Let me see. (*Snatches sketch book.*) You can't draw! Why are you trying to draw when you can't draw? Suddenly everybody imagines he's an artist!

RODERIGUES. The very old like him should be kept apart from the very young like me. I can see it now.

SHYLOCK. Stop squabbling. Moses can begin without Jessica,

and Signor Usque has promised to tell us about his new play.

MOSES. Another one! Suddenly! Everyone! An artist!

USQUE. It will be a debate.

SHYLOCK. Between whom?

USQUE. Between rabbis who were interpreting —

SHYLOCK. — the interpretations of the interpretations of the great scholars who interpreted the meaning of the meaning —

USQUE. Precisely! You will remember that Catherine of Aragon had been the widow of Henry the Eighth's dead brother, Arthur, and now Henry wanted his marraige with her annulled. The Pope would probably have said yes, but was worried about Catherine's nephew, Charles V. Both — Henry and the pope, that is — found support for their views in the Bible.

SHYLOCK. Naturally!

USQUE. Henry's wishes were supported by the book of Leviticus which said marriage to the widow of a dead brother was forbidden. While Rome's refusal supported itself with Deuteronomy which allows such a marriage in the case of a previously childless match.

SHYLOCK. Sons! Sons must be born to perpetuate the man's name! Power, lineage, lust — and all rushing for succour to the Bible.

USQUE. But the problem of interpretation was perplexing.

SHYLOCK. Naturally!

USQUE. And so to whom did they turn for guidance?

SHYLOCK. We can't wait to hear.

MOSES. To the bickering old Jews of Venice.

SHYLOCK. *You* know?

MOSES. Around 1530. Big quarrels.

RIVKA. Old fools of Venice, more like.

MOSES. And all a lot of nonsense. There was a man I remember

came all the way from England to get the opinions of the
Italian Rabbis —

RIVKA. Who immediately formed different camps!

MOSES. Now what was his name — er — er —

USQUE. Richard Cooke.

MOSES. Cooke. Yes. Names! Why can't I remember names?

RIVKA. They didn't know the King of England or the Pope but
they fought for them!

MOSES. I used to remember everybody's names. Age!

RIVKA. Old fools!

MOSES. Damn age!

USQUE. But, who do *you* think was right, Shylock? Remember
my play will not be seeking interpretations of history, but of
the scriptures.

JESSICA *enters and takes up her pose the other side of*
SHYLOCK.

SHYLOCK. You're late.

JESSICA. This is the last time I sit, father.

SHYLOCK. Don't you understand how insulting it is to be late
for an appointment?

JESSICA. Signor Castelazzo was not held up by me.

SHYLOCK. This is my house, and while under my roof —

JESSICA (*challengingly*). While under your roof, *what?*

SHYLOCK. An appointment is sacred.

JESSICA. You exaggerate.

SHYLOCK. To keep another waiting is to say to him you don't
care for him.

JESSICA. Or that you care more for what you've left. Or that
what you've left presented problems unanticipated. Or that
what you've left was a dying man, you were needed, or you
were compelled, or forced — really! Father! You're so full of
tight, restricting little codes.

SHYLOCK. An appointment is a bond. Between two people. They depend upon each other honouring it, and if it's broken — lives can be affected, deals fall through, hearts broken, disappointment —

JESSICA. The scheme of things! The scheme of things! Stop lecturing me with your scheme of things.

MOSES. I have a painting to paint. Please.

USQUE. You've not answered my questions, Signor Shylock.

SHYLOCK. Ask my daughter. She's the clever one.

USQUE. My new play, about a quarrel between rabbis, some interpreting Deuteronomy on behalf of the Papacy, others Leviticus on behalf of Henry the Eighth. The positions were this —

JESSICA. With respect, Signor Usque, I don't need to have their relative positions described. The idea is offensive. To scurry backwards and forwards in and out of the Bible's pages for such an obscene quarrel — the Rabbis should have been ashamed of themselves. The cause doesn't interest me.

USQUE. The cause doesn't interest me, either, but the nature of interpretation does.

SHYLOCK (*but proud*). Forgive her. She's had good tutors to exercise her mind but no mother to shape her manners.

RODERIGUES (*sketching furiously*). But keep her angry, she looks beautiful when she's angry. Beautiful!

MOSES. Idiot!

RIVKA. I thought women today only looked beautiful when they were in love, Roderigues.

JESSICA (*topping her*). This is the last time I pose, father.

SHYLOCK. You've told me already.

JESSICA. As you've told me a thousand times that this is your house and your roof.

SHYLOCK. Under which you are deprived of nothing.

JESSICA. Except the sweetness of feeling that it is *my* house and *my* roof also. You want a debate for your play, Signor Usque? Then debate this question: to whom does a house belong? Only the father? Not even the mother? And if not the children and the mother, then how must their relationship be described? As temporary occupants? As long standing visitors? At what point is the child's right of movement and taste taken into consideration? Does she only become whole when taken from the possession of her father to the possession of her husband? What do Leviticus and Deuteronomy have to say on those things? Look how my father swells with pride at his daughter's intellect. He's given me teachers to nourish and exercise my mind, while he continues to exercise control.

SHYLOCK. If she is talking about control and the child's right it can only mean she wants to go out again one day soon. I feel her tremors long before she erupts.

JESSICA. He talks as though the world elected him.

SHYLOCK. *She* talks as though the tutors' fees were well spent!

JESSICA. Tell him his daughter must be taken seriously.

SHYLOCK. Tell her she should not be neglecting her music studies.

JESSICA. Tell him you can be oppressed by study.

SHYLOCK. Dancing, singing, the instruments I bought for her — tell her.

JESSICA. Tell him not everyone wants to perform, some are content to listen.

SHYLOCK. Tell her —

JESSICA. Tell her, tell her! Tell her nothing more —

She storms out. SHYLOCK *is shocked.*

RIVKA. Mean! Mean! To withhold praise from your daughter, mean. From your own daughter.

SHYLOCK. The Talmud says: praise not a man more than ten per cent of his worth.

USQUE. Forgive me, Signor Shylock, I do not think you've

judged well. You'll drive her into a hasty marriage.

RIVKA. He doesn't *want* her to marry.

USQUE *turns to* SHYLOCK *for a response.*

SHYLOCK. The *pope* calls for the vows of chastity, but *God*
only ever ordained matrimony. To whom should I listen?
(*But he is thinking of other things.*)

Scene Six

ANTONIO's *house.*
Present are BASSANIO, LORENZO *and* GRAZIANO. *They
have just eaten.*
SHYLOCK *has been with them but is out of the room,
unwell, accompanied by* ANTONIO.
*Contented pause of men who've eaten, drunk and conversed
well.*

GRAZIANO. Well, the poor Jew is very sick, for sure. He's been
gone a quarter of an hour.

BASSANIO. I think you gave him too much wine.

LORENZO. Or the food was too rich for him.

BASSANIO. The man looked anxious. Worried. Sad.

GRAZIANO. I must say, he did drink fast. Very nervously. He
came in and at once downed two glasses of wine.

LORENZO. It was not that. He eats and drinks and talks at the
same time. There's no grace in the man.

BASSANIO. I find him most interesting. *You* see many Jews in
Venice — at least ten thousand, I'd say —

GRAZIANO. Fourteen hundred.

BASSANIO. Really? As few as that? Well, they seem more. But
where I lived, just ouside Milan, we saw none. Everyone
talked about them, but I'd never actually met one. So for me
— interesting.

SHYLOCK *and* ANTONIO *enter.*

SHYLOCK. Oh, I love Venice.

GRAZIANO. A noble city, Signor Shylock, you're right.

LORENZO. You were born here, of course.

SHYLOCK. Yes, I was born here, of course.

LORENZO. I ask because so many of you come from here and there and everywhere.

SHYLOCK. I know why you ask.

LORENZO. It must be very difficult for your tribe to produce much of art or thought, as civilized nations do who have roots in territory.

SHYLOCK. Very.

LORENZO. Would you not agree that —

SHYLOCK, *bored and despising* LORENZO, *turns aside to talk with his friend,* ANTONIO. *He's still a little drunk.*

SHYLOCK. I love Venice, Antonio, because it's a city full of men busy living, and passing through, and free to do both as their right, not as a favour.

ANTONIO. Venice is distorted through your gratitude, Shylock, you've forgotten your yellow hat.

SHYLOCK. If I'd been a damned physician, I'd not have to wear this damned yellow hat every time I took a walk. Physician! Now *there* was a profession to belong to instead of my own seedy lineage. Failures! (*Pause.*) I descended from German Jews, you know. My grandparents. Grubby little things from Cologne. Came to Venice as small-time money lenders for the poor. But my parents — they tried a new profession. Very brave. Second-hand clothing! My mother went blind patching up smelly old clothes and my father became famous for beating out, cleaning and reconditioning old mattresses. Bringers of sleep — not a dishonourable trade don't you think, gentlemen? Mattresses; bringers of sweet sleep.

LORENZO. And sweet plagues.

SHYLOCK (*hisses*). Yes! I know! Better than you, I know! (*Relaxing again.*) But he was not an ambitious man, my

father. Had no confidence in himself. Not like the really big
pawnbrokers, men who built up huge stores of carvings,
furniture, paintings. Tintorettos would pass through *their*
hands while stained pantaloons passed through my father's.
And for their banquets the dukes could always be certain of
hiring dazzling tapestry in the Ghetto. Except from my
father. Verminous vests you could get from him.

LORENZO. It's true. The Ghetto *is* notorious for its smells.

ANTONIO. I will not have discourtesies in my house.

LORENZO. You must forgive me, Signor Antonio. But I too am
a guest, and we can't pretend that animosity doesn't exist
between your guests. You ask me to respect your Jewish
friend but what respect has he shown for me? Respect has no
merit if it's unilateral. And disputation is a sacred right in our
city. On several occasions this evening I've attempted to
engage Signor Shylock in a theological discussion. He's
turned away. If courtesy is esteemed then such a manner is
not an efficacious way to achieve it.

SHYLOCK. Efficacious! Unilateral! Disputation! What a rich
vocabulary! Perhaps I'm too frightened to dispute with you,
friend Lorenzo. Yours is a university trained mind. Mine is
the Ghetto's.

BASSANIO. You must not be surprised if with such scorn you
attract hostility.

LORENZO (*with evangelist fervour*). 'They are not humbled
even unto this day, neither have they feared, nor walked in
my law, nor in my statues, that I have set before you and
before your fathers.' Thus sayeth Ezekiel.

SHYLOCK. It was Jeremiah. Oh dear. You want theological
disputation? Listen. You have us for life, gentlemen, for life.
Learn to live with us. The Jew is the Christian's parent.
Difficult, I know. Parent-children relationships, always
difficult, and even worse when murder is involved within the
family. But what can we do? It *is* the family! Not only *would*
I be your friend but I *have* to be your friend. Don't scowl,
Signor sweet Christian. For life. Old Shylock, Jew of Venice.

For ever! The prophets, perseverance, protest, account books and all!

Long embarrassed pause.

GRAZIANO. Yes. Well. A very noble city. You are absolutely right, Shylock. We were discussing nobility the other night.

SHYLOCK. Now what is he talking about?

GRAZIANO. Nobility and power. What *is* the nature of nobility and in what does power reside?

SHYLOCK. Power? Were we talking about power?

GRAZIANO. Bassanio here believes that power resides in our ability to trade.

BASSANIO. Lorenzo-the-silent on the other hand believes power resides in the strength of moral superiority. Only Christian principle should activate our republic.

SHYLOCK. Good God! There was no one in the room when I was talking!

BASSANIO. While Graziano here believes power resides in the family who trades, which power in turn gives the family nobility.

GRAZIANO. Exactly! The *accumulated* knowledge of superiority *gives* one superiority: Venice is as a second Rome.

ANTONIO. Venice as a second Rome is nonsense. We're a commercial enterprise and no more.

BASSANIO. Come, Antonio, that's cynicism. I agree in part but that's not the whole truth. What about Venetian rule of law? Her Christian pride and fervour? All vital organs of the Empire.

ANTONIO. The most vital organs of our Empire are warehouses, ships' holds, barges and pack-horses. We're not even honest industrialists, we're simply importers and exporters, rich because the commerce of other people flows through us, not because we produce it ourselves. And as for Venice's sense of justice, it's to retain for her patricians the best opportunities for long-distance trade. Our motives are opportunist and our power rests on a geographical accident, so let's have no nonsense about Venice being a second Rome.

SHYLOCK. No, no, friend Antonio. Forgive me, I must quarrel with you as well. Oh, this is terrible. You defend me and I cross you. But I must. You both miss the point of Venice, of all Italy. Venice as Rome or not, as a commercial enterprise or not is irrelevant. What you say may be true but there is a scheme of things much grander. Let me remind you of three distinct developments affecting the history of this extraordinary land of yours and let's see where real power resides.

LORENZO. Are we now to be given a history lesson about our own lands by a German Jew?

SHYLOCK. Don't be offended, Lorenzo-the-silent. Remember, the synagogue existed in Rome before the Papacy.

GRAZIANO (*incredulous*). The rabbi before the pope?

SHYLOCK. The Roman wars. Jewish slaves. The princes of Israel. Now ssssh! And listen. It's a very thrilling story. Three developments! But first, who said: 'Religionem imperare non possumus —

ANTONIO. — quia nemo cogitur —

SHYLOCK. — ut credat invitus'? Mmm? How do you like my pronunciation of Latin, eh?

GRAZIANO. 'We cannot enforce acceptance of a creed, since no one can be compelled to believe against his will.'

SHYLOCK. Excellent, Graziano, bravo!

GRAZIANO. Had to learn it by heart at school.

SHYLOCK. But who said it?

Pause.

ANTONIO. Cassiodorus!

SHYLOCK. The last and lovely link between Imperial Rome and Gothic Italy.

ANTONIO. Born 479, died 575.

Then SHYLOCK *tells his story with mounting excitement and theatricality, using whatever is around him for props, moving furniture, food, perhaps even people, like men on his chessboard of history.* ANTONIO *is singled out to be 'Cassiodorus'.*

SHYLOCK. A sweet and intellectual man. Dubious elasticity of conscience, perhaps — always able to make himself necessary to the different rulers of the country, but still. A statesman! A scholar! And for what is this man remembered most? His administrations on behalf of monarchs? Never! And here is development one. At sixty he retired from politics and *then,* only then began his real life's work.

And *what* was this work, gentlemen, for another thirty-six years until he died aged *ninety-six?* (*Pause.*) During his life he'd succeeded in preserving through all the devastations of civil wars and foreign invasions, a great collection of Greek and Roman classic manuscripts, which, during his retirement to Bruttii, he made certain were scrupulously copied by the monks. *What* a work! What a faith! But why? Why should he have bothered? What makes one man so cherish the work of others that he lovingly guards it, copies, preserves it? And a Christian, too, preserving the works of pagans! I love it! From monastery to monastery, especially among the Benedictines, busy, busy, scribbling, for centuries, until the book trade creeps from the monasteries into the universities. The scholars take over from the monks. The pattern takes shape. Development number two: the destruction of the Roman Empire! Italy breaks into three pieces. The north goes to the German Holy Roman Empire, the centre becomes dominated by the Papacy, and the French house of Anjou takes over the South. Look how fortunes change, rearrange themselves.

LORENZO. Your pleasure in history is superficial, signor — playful. Its patterns please you but not its meanings. How can you expect us to listen seriously to your analysis? Such delight in chance is spiteful. You'd have us believe there was no cause and effect. I have no sympathy with such approaches.

SHYLOCK. Aha! Spirit! I might even come to respect you, young man, but —

LORENZO. And don't play with me, either, signor.

SHYLOCK. But — you read me wrong if you believe I read history so carelessly. I'm perfectly aware how causes work their effects — but *within their time*. The line *I* stretch joins together men and moments who could never possibly have forecast one another's acts. Did old Cassiodorus working away in the year 539 see how Italy's development would shape? Hear me out. It's thrilling, thrilling — believe me.

   The land in three pieces, then. But does everything stand still? Impossible! Watch in the north how the German Holy Roman Empire disintegrates; in the centre how the families of Rome brawl among themselves; in the south how the French house of Anjou fights the Spanish house of Aragon. Nothing stands still! And as the dust of war and madness settles all is revealed! The northern half of the peninsular fragmented! And into what? Into what, gentlemen? City States! The magnificent City States of Milan, Genoa, Florence, Venice! The Empires have broken up, and suddenly — every city is left to its own government. What can it do? How *does* one govern? Industry and trade grows. Can't help itself. What! The centre of the Mediterranean basin and *not* trade? So — it begins! The Italians invent partnership agreements, holding companies, marine insurance, credit transfers, double-entry book-keeping! Progress! But listen! Listen what else happened in the fourteenth century, and don't forget old Cassiodorus lurking away patiently down there in the sixth century. More business meant more complex agreements, which meant more law, which complicated the business of government, which meant men of greater education were needed, which meant a *new* kind of education, more practical, more — ah! worldly! And where, where I ask you, could that worldly, new education come from to produce that new law, the new government? Tell me. (*Pause.*) Why, from books! Where else? And where *were* the books? Old Cassiodorus! In the monasteries! He'd preserved the ancient manuscripts of Rome and Greece, hallelujah! Praise be to wise old men!

Aren't you enjoying it? Admit it, doesn't it thrill you to watch it take shape? Be generous. Let yourselves go, for here comes development three. The year 1450. Two beautiful births: a wily old German from Mayence named Gutenberg gives birth to an extraordinary invention called — the printing press: and a great classical scholar named Aldus Manutius is born. Here! In our very own city of Venice, at the age of forty-five, less than a hundred years ago, the great Manutius sets up his divine press and produces the incredible Aldine Editions. Suddenly — everybody can possess a book! And what books! The works of — Plato, Homer, Pindar and Aristophanes, Xenophon, Seneca, Plutarch and Sophocles, Aristotle, Lysias, Euripides, Demosthenes, Thucydides, Herodotus, and all printed from manuscripts kept and preserved in monasteries as far apart as Sweden and Constantinople which Italians were now bringing back home. Amazing! Knowledge, like underground springs, fresh and constantly there, till one day — up! Bubbling! For dying men to drink, for survivors from dark and terrible times. I love it! When generals imagine their vain glory is all, and demagogues smile with sweet benevolence as they tighten their screws of power — up! Up bubbles the little spring. Bubble, bubble, bubble! A little, little lost spring, full of blinding questions and succulent doubts. The word! Unsuspected! Written! Printed! Indestructible! Boom! I love it!

Bells ring. Time to return to the Ghetto. ANTONIO *rises to give* SHYLOCK *his yellow hat. He looks at* ANTONIO *and shrugs sadly, as though the hat is evidence to refute all he's said.*

ANTONIO. What little lost spring can help you now?

And yet . . . he defiantly places it on his head, embraces ANTONIO, *bows to the other three and goes off chuckling and mumbling . . .*

SHYLOCK. Bubble, bubble, bubble! Bubble, bubble, bubble! Bubble bubble . . .

ACT TWO

Scene One

Belmont. PORTIA's *estate outside Venice.*
The estate is in great disrepair. PORTIA *and her maid,*
NERISSA, *both in simple, hardwearing clothes, have just arrived*
to view the neglect.

PORTIA. Decided! The speculating days of the family Contarini
are done. The goods warehoused in our name at Beirut and
Famagusta we'll sell of cheaply to cut our losses, I shall raise
what I can from the sale of our properties on Crete, Corfu
and the Dalmatian towns which are too far from Venice and
not worth their troubles, but —

NERISSA. — but agriculture, my lady, what does my lady
Portia know of agriculture?

PORTIA. Your lady Portia will learn, Nerissa. The famines are
cruel and constant visitors. We must reclaim the land. Besides,
the competition for the trade routes is too devious a task for
my taste, and —

NERISSA. — and pirates are in the Adriatic, we know all that,
my lady, most demoralising for our sailors, but —

PORTIA. Antwerp! Seville! London! Too far!

NERISSA. — but to leave the city?

PORTIA. I love my city, Nerissa, but I hear rumours. Timber is
scarce, the number of ships registered by Venice is dropping.
Signs, my dear, the signs are there. It's goodbye to Venice,
and into the wheatlands of my estates near Treviso and
Vicenza and here, Belmont. We'll become growers!
Stock-breeders! Cattle and drainage! that's where our

our fortunes will go.

NERISSA. When you've realised them, that is.

PORTIA. The land! I've decided! (*Pause.*) Good God! (*Looking around.*) What a mess my father's made of my childhood! (*Pause.*) Is this the room?

NERISSA. Facing the sun at eleven o'clock. This is it.

PORTIA. And *here* we are to find the caskets?

NERISSA (*searching*). Here, somewhere in all this neglect. Your father's puzzle for picking a spouse. One gold, one silver, one lead. (NERISSA *reveals a dusty corner.*) Found! 'By his choice shall you know him.'

PORTIA. What an inheritance! Ten estates in ruin, and a foolish philosophic whim for to find me an idiot husband. Oh father, father, father! What *were* you thinking of? Hear me up there. I will honour the one wish you uttered: whom the casket chooses, I'll marry. But your rules for judging men I will forget, and these ruins will be put back again. The material things of this world count. We *have* no soul without labour, and labour I will, father, hear me.

She begins to move about the room pulling down tattered curtains, replacing furniture on its feet, picking up strewn books, perhaps rubbing encrusted dirt from a vase till its frieze can be seen, but moving, moving.

NERISSA. How your mother would love to be alive now, with all this possibility of work at last.

PORTIA. Perhaps that's my real inheritance, Nerissa: father's marriage to a peasant. My energy is hers.

NERISSA. And such energy, madame.

PORTIA. All stored and waiting for the poor man's death.

NERISSA. Come, be just. He didn't commit you in marriage at the age of seven as my father did. He gave you tutors.

PORTIA. Ah, thank heaven for them.

NERISSA. A very strange collection, I used to think.

PORTIA. The crippled Ochino from Padua for mathematics,

the boring Lamberti from Genoa for history.

NERISSA. The handsome Mansueti from Florence for Greek and philosophy . . .

PORTIA. And for Hebrew, Abraham Cardorso, the sad, old Jewish mystic from the Ghetto Nuovo. I am indebted to them all.

NERISSA. Why in God's name did you want to learn Hebrew, my lady?

PORTIA. To read the words of the prophets in the language they were spoken, why else? Meanings change when men translate them into other tongues. Oh! Those caskets! Those stupid caskets! Take them out of my sight. I loved him dearly, my father, but those caskets will bring me down as his other madnesses brought down my mother, I feel it.

NERISSA. *Such* energy, madame, you tire me to watch you.

PORTIA. And you must have it too, Nerissa. I demand it. You are not only my help but my friend and I'll have you educated and protected from the miseries of an ill-chosen marriage.

NERISSA. If, that is, you can protect yourself from one.

PORTIA. True! My God, and what suitors have announced they're coming. Why, do you wonder, *is* there such interest in me?

NERISSA. Riches, madame, riches, riches, riches.

PORTIA. But my riches are potential, not realised.

NERISSA. The family name?

PORTIA. My family name is illustrious but somewhat moth-eaten.

NERISSA. Your beauty.

PORTIA. No flattery. I won't have it. My beauty is, well — it *is*, but no more than many such women of Venice I could name.

NERISSA. Why, then? *You* say.

PORTIA. I *think* I know, but it's not certain. There are simply

— mmm — pulses in my veins. I feel, I feel — I feel I-am-the-
new-woman-and-they-know-me-not! For centuries the
Church has kept me comfortably comforting and cooking
and pleasing and patient. And now — Portia is no longer
patient. Yes, she can spin, weave, sew. Give her meat and
drink — she can dress them. Show her flax and wool — she
can make you clothes. But — Portia reads! Plato and
Aristotle, Ovid and Catullus, all in the original! Latin, Greek,
Hebrew —

NERISSA. With difficulty!

PORTIA. She has read history and politics, she has studied logic
and mathematics, astronomy and geography, she has
conversed with liberal minds on the nature of the soul, the
efficacy of religious freedom, the very existence of God!

NERISSA. Why! Her brain can hardly catch its breath!

PORTIA. She has observed, judged, organised and — crept out
of the kitchen. Knowledge of love and corruption and evil
may have lost her sweet innocence but — the fireside chair
rocks without her now, and what she will do is a mystery.
Portia is a new woman, Nerissa. There is a woman on the
English throne. Anything can happen and they are coming to
find out.

Scene Two

A room in Belmont. Time has passed. Some order is restored.
PORTIA and BASSANIO in conversation. NERISSA reading.

BASSANIO. Wrong, madame, wrong! It may be true that trade
in spices and the old wares is less profitable and safe these
days, but land and agriculture are not where the fortunes lie.
Precious metals! Trade in those. Gold! A bank! The bank of
Contarini! — doesn't that thought dazzle you? Besides, where
will you obtain your capital for implements?

PORTIA. I've sold estates, and will perhaps sell even more with
your help, but now dear friend, you must choose. Choose
wisely. None of the others did. Some chose swiftly, some
with pride. Others stood thinking for so long they terrified

themselves out of the simple ability to choose at all. So take your place and take your time. I'll talk with Nerissa. She's reading the letters of Seneca and I've asked her to select a favourite one. I think I know which one it will be.

BASSANIO *takes up his place by the caskets.* NERISSA *approaches* PORTIA.

NERISSA. This one, my lady, letter forty-seven. (*She begins to read.*) 'I'm glad to hear, from these people who've been visiting you, that you live on friendly terms with your slaves. It is just what one expects of an enlightened, cultivated person like yourself . . .'

Her voice lowers as the main melody takes over. Attention must be focused upon BASSANIO.

BASSANIO. What an eccentric test of love. Whose mind constructed this? 'By his choice shall you know him.' (*Contemptuously, and gradually drawn into a conversation with* PORTIA'S FATHER *'up there'.*) What shall you know of him? That if he choose gold he will be a man without a soul, with a purse where his heart should be? But a man without a soul may have cunning, surely? Greed does not preclude perception, and a greedy man may well detect misfortune where his instinct leads. Suppose an even more human condition: the man who loves gold has plagues of guilt and so is ripe for self-disgust? Now there's a man who'd shy away from the shiny stuff. No, I don't see the point of such a simple trick. And silver? What's one supposed to think of that, stuck between gold and lead? Oh, here's the mediocre man! Here's the man plays safe with life and neither dares much nor achieves! Or is silver the test of the temperate man, the sober man? Perhaps the diplomat is being looked for here? The statesman? The judge? Not unworthy men! Yet I'm hardly any of those. A little bit of each in me I'd like to think, but — I hardly riot in those qualities. Still, if such a man is wanted for that extraordinary lady, and that extraordinary lady is what I want, then perhaps the statesman, diplomat and judge in me had *better* blossom. Hm! Not such a simple test after all. Come on now, Bassanio, use your wits. You've not survived this far without an arsenal

of guile. Think! Think! What father, wanting his daughter to
marry a statesman, diplomat or judge would devise such a
scheme? A very wise father I'd say, if I didn't know that he
was very stupid. Perhaps, then, a better question would be:
does Portia look the kind of a daughter who'd have the kind
of father would *want* her to marry a statesman, diplomat or
judge? (*Pause.*) I will go mad.

The wrong approach! These caskets can't be a test for a
profession but — a sort, a kind, a spirit. The question then is:
what kind of, sort of spirit would such a woman's father
want for her? The father! Look to the father. He's the key.
Good! That's something. So. The father descends from a
long illustrious line. An aristocracy. But by the time the
blood of rulers reached her father it had been watered down
to the blood of a philosopher. And now, abundant though
the estates' possibilities are, yet they're in ruin. Very
decorous ruin, but — ruin. What metal would a ruined
ruinous philosopher choose? (*Long pause, smile, he's seen
through the strategy, but at first cunningly misleads.*) There
can only be one answer. Simple! The end of philosophy is
despair. He looked around him, saw the constant battles
being fought, the waste, disintegration and decay, and he
concluded: for my daughter, none of that! Gold! The hard,
determined, merciless pursuit of gain, security and comfort.
Gold! With gold is bought beauty, art, obedience, the power
for good. Gold! For my daughter shall be trapped a man of
gold. The sun is golden, the harvest too — energy and
sustenance. These things I will, for my only child, these
things which I with my engagement in philosophy neglected
to provide. Gold! (*Pause.*) And then he changed his mind!
For who can change the habits of a foolish lifetime? (*To*
PORTIA.) Lead, my lady. Lead I choose. My brain has
battled. There's its choice.

PORTIA. Your brain, Bassanio? Not your heart? Still, heart or
brain, you've chosen as my father wished.

BASSANIO. Not you?

PORTIA. I? You must forgive me. It *is* possible for eyes to
meet and feel their love at once, I know. But I'm not made

that way. Love grows with me. My mother taught love
ripens on the mind, is made of passions, laughter, all the
minutiae of living *shared* rather than surmised. Is that
pedantic, you think? Would you rather I embrace you now
and say, with routine ardour, that *your* choice decides?
Don't think from my response that I'm a calculating woman,
though sometimes I wish I were. The truth is I'm impulsive.
My responses shape at once. I know a man, a situation at a
glance, but my mother said 'humility, your impulse may be
wrong'. You'd rather have my love relaxed and confident,
Bassanio? Be patient. We will live together. All I have is yours,
you know that. Settle here. Rehearse the role of husband.
We'll work together, find each other carefully. We *may* be
born for one another, part of me believes we are. I want my
all to know it though. See, I'm trembling as I talk. I think
you must embrace me after all.

They embrace.

Now leave. I must arrange and scheme for you.

BASSANIO (*facilely*). I have no words.

PORTIA (*catching the tone, cools*). I'm touched.

BASSANIO *leaves.*

Perhaps I should be his mistress only. That gives him no
holds over me then. As his wife the State chains me. *There's*
something to exercise your logic on, Nerissa.

NERISSA. You're uncertain?

PORTIA. Oh, I am that.

NERISSA. You should not love someone you don't like.

PORTIA. What a ridiculous carrier of passion — a casket. I'm
uncertain all right. What if I should tire of him? God forbid a
woman should tire of a man. Of his vanities and little faults
which always, always magnify with time. He has such a
blindness for his image, such an incredible satisfaction with
his long-considered thimbleful of thoughts, his firm decisive
manner over that which should be racked with doubts, his —
his — his silly coloured feathers which he feels to be his
masculinity. Oh! his masculinity!

NERISSA. Have you watched the way a man walks? As though balancing a cannon-ball on each shoulder, careful that the width of him is seen, felt?

PORTIA. There is such presumption in him, such an air of arrogance, as though what else could woman be but his rib, a mere bone of his body. After all, my dear, men have won battles with a bone missing!

NERISSA (*ribaldly*). And lost many even with one there.

Great laughter between them.

PORTIA. Heaven help us, but there are so few poets among them!

NERISSA. They are such clumsy things. So weighed down with dull earthiness.

PORTIA. Except at wooing-time, and then, ah! Then — have you noted that collapse of features which they feel is tenderness? That slow softening of the eyes into a milky melancholy they think is love-sick helplessness?

NERISSA. That sudden clenching of the jaw and fist which struggles to be passion?

PORTIA. What feeble and pathetic arts they have. And we must pretend! Poor gimcrack men! Oh! There are such stirrings in me. Such untried intellect. Such marvellous loves and wisdom. I could found cities with my strengths, Nerissa, cities undreamed of by any man.

Bells peal out as we change to —

Scene Three

The 'logetta' beneath the campanile of St. Mark's. Normally a meeting-place for patricians.
     TUBAL *and* RODERIGUES *approach from different parts. It is night.*

TUBAL. Nothing?

RODERIGUES. Nothing!

TUBAL. You've asked discreetly?

RODERIGUES. Discreetly and indiscreetly. What do I care now!

TUBAL. The entire Ghetto is out looking for her, taking risks. Foolish girl.

RODERIGUES. 'I know your daughter,' I told him, I warned him.

TUBAL. You warned? I warned! Who didn't warn?

RODERIGUES. 'She's too intelligent to be constrained, too old to be teased and too hot to be predictable,' I told him.

TUBAL. Foolish girl!

RODERIGUES. But he understands nothing. 'If I'd beaten her, been a drunkard, gambled my money away like those other old men, playing cards and dice all day between synagogue services . . . But we loved one another!' As if loving helps!

TUBAL. Nor is that to be his only tribulation. There are other calamities in the wind. The sea's wind. Your clever patron signed a bond with his best friend, Antonio. It was to be a joke, to mock the laws of Venice: a loan of three thousand ducats with a pound of flesh as bond if, within three months, the loan was not repaid. And now —

RODERIGUES. A pound of flesh?

TUBAL. And now his ships are threatened.

RODERIGUES. A pound of flesh?

TUBAL. A pound of flesh, his ships in threat, the Ghetto penniless, and the time is up at six the evening after tomorrow.

RODERIGUES. A pound of *human* flesh?

TUBAL. Yes, yes, yes, YES!

RODERIGUES. But, of course, the ships are not sunk.

TUBAL. No! Captured only! By pirates. The market is buzzing with the news.

RODERIGUES. And the bond is a joke.

TUBAL. There are no more jokes left in this world, Roderigues.

The next, perhaps — ach! I am so loath to lend and deal in this trade any more.

Enter GRAZIANO.

GRAZIANO. Ah, signor Tubal, if anyone knows where Antonio is, it will be you.

RODERIGUES. Here comes everyman's everything and I'm in no mood for him.

TUBAL. What's the news of Antonio's ships?

GRAZIANO. Bad, bad, bad, oh bad.

TUBAL. Bad, we know. Facts we want.

GRAZIANO (*cheekily*). The facts are that the news is bad.

TUBAL (*with powerful anger*). No courtesies and games. Tell us the news.

GRAZIANO (*portentously*). Grave. The news is grave. In view of how huge the cargo is the maritime office have ordered armed ships to the rescue.

TUBAL. Good, that's news worth taking back. Come, Roderigues.

GRAZIANO. But the damn winds are not helping, they fear a storm. The armed ships are paralysed.

TUBAL. Oh, Abraham! Abraham! Someone's God is angry. I'm too old for all this, too old, too old . . .

TUBAL *and* RODERIGUES *leave.*

GRAZIANO (*mocking as he, too, leaves*). Oh Abraham, Abraham! I'm too old for all this, too old, too old . . .

LORENZO *and* JESSICA *who have been looking for each other now meet, clutch one another in relief. She is agitated.*

LORENZO. You're trembling.

JESSICA. I'm frightened and I'm ashamed, so I'm trembling.

LORENZO. Oh, those eyes. Those sad, sad eyes.

JESSICA. Forget my eyes, Lorenzo, and tell me what is to happen next.

LORENZO. First be calm, if for no other reason than not to command the staring of others.

JESSICA. I've spent so much, you see. It's cost so much.

LORENZO. I know, I know.

JESSICA. The decision to break away. You can't imagine. To be cut off.

LORENZO. I know.

JESSICA. So I'm drained. I'll be all right soon but for the next hours my reason is numb and you must do it all.

LORENZO. Trust me.

JESSICA. Kiss me.

He hesitates.

All these months of meetings and you've not kissed me.

He hesitates again.

Haven't you kissed a woman before?

LORENZO. A hand, a cheek.

JESSICA. Not lips?

LORENZO. Not lips.

JESSICA. Then mine will be the first for you.

LORENZO. And mine?

JESSICA. Will be the first for me.

They kiss.

Oh, I have known that kiss all my life.

LORENZO (*lifting her and whirling her round*). Now, I would like to nail your name, proclaim you, claim you!

JESSICA. And say this is mine, and this, and here I've been before, and that skin, that smell, that touch so belongs, belongs, belongs that surely I was born the twin to it.

LORENZO. Nail your name and claim your strength!

They kiss as SHYLOCK's voice is heard.

Scene Four

SHYLOCK's *study. He's trying to read a letter from his daughter.*

SHYLOCK. 'Dear Father. I am not what you would like me to be, and what I am, brings me to this. To write more will urge upon me the necessity to think more. I have thought and reassured enough, not conclusively, but sufficient to drive me out. Reflect on our quarrels. They have said all. Your daughter, Jessica.'

RIVKA *enters.*

RIVKA. And where has your joking got you?

SHYLOCK. I have a letter from my daughter, now be silent, Rivka.

RIVKA. Have you asked yourself why she's gone?

SHYLOCK. I'm trying to find out, don't nag at me.

RIVKA. Are you certain there was no wrong in *you*?

SHYLOCK. You're the only person I know who *asks* accusations.

RIVKA. Please, Shylock, I beg you. Be a kind man, be a considerate brother. I've no health for laughter. Be finished with joking.

SHYLOCK. I have a letter from my daughter.

RIVKA. You've read it seven times, already. Talk with me. I'm not a fool.

SHYLOCK. What would you have me talk about, sister?

RIVKA. The meaning of your bond.

SHYLOCK. It has meanings? Clauses, perhaps, but meanings?

RIVKA. Clauses, meanings, meanings, clauses! If *you* won't read the meanings like a man, then this old woman will. What you wanted to mock now mocks you! That's what your bond means.

SHYLOCK. I don't see what meaning that meaning means.

RIVKA. Oh yes you do.

SHYLOCK. I see problems. I see possibilities. I see maybes and perhapses. The problem of Antonio's ships captured, the possibility of rescue, though maybe the wind will delay it or perhaps Antonio's creditors will advance him more money and there'll be no problem because he'll have the possibility to repay me in time.

RIVKA. In time? What time? The clocks will soon strike six and that will only leave one day.

SHYLOCK. I have a letter from my daughter. Please.

RIVKA. I know you know the meanings that I mean. You're wriggling so.

SHYLOCK. I must hear this nonsense through I suppose.

RIVKA. Don't be rude to me, Shylock! You have a friend. Good. A gentile and gentle man. Good. You made some peace for yourself. I was happy for you. Good. But could you leave it like that, my wise man, always throwing his voice, his ideas about, on this, on that, here, there, to anyone, could you leave it well alone like that? Oh Shylock, my young brother. I've watched you, wandering away from Jewish circles, putting your nose out in alien places. I've watched you be restless and pretend you can walk in anybody's streets. Don't think I've not understood you; suffocating in this little yard, waiting for your very own scholar to arrive. It made me ache to watch you, looking for moral problems to sharpen your mind, for disputations — as if there weren't enough troubles inside these peeling walls. But you *can't* pretend you're educated, just as you can't pretend you're not an alien or that this Ghetto has no walls. Pretend, pretend, pretend! All your life! Wanting to be what you're not. Imagining the world as you want. And now, again, as always, against all reason, this mad pretence that Antonio's ships will come in safe. (*Pause.*) You've mocked their law.

SHYLOCK. Which mocked at us.

RIVKA. A hero! Shylock to the defence of his people. Can't you see what you've done?

SHYLOCK. Asserted dignity, that's what I've done.

RIVKA. That? That's what you've done? Nothing else? (*Pause.*) To assert the dignity of your mocked people you have chained your friend's life to a mocking bond, *that's* what you've done.

SHYLOCK. Go to your room, Rivka, you're becoming excited.

RIVKA. Shylock! Go and find the money! Knock on every Ghetto door, beg, plead, bully — but get it. Now. Before it's too late.

SHYLOCK. Foolish woman. Do you think I haven't tried? The Ghetto is drained. The last tax emptied every purse.

RIVKA. Then let him borrow from his friends.

SHYLOCK. They don't trust his future now.

RIVKA. Then don't you know the court will relieve you of your bond to save a citizen's life?

SHYLOCK. Tomorrow. Tomorrow we'll talk about it.

RIVKA. They will even let you bend the law and lend him further ducats for repayment when the hour is passed.

SHYLOCK. Rivka, please.

RIVKA. But not everyone in the Ghetto will agree to the bending of the law, will they? And that's where your moral problem begins. You can't see that?

SHYLOCK. Please, Rivka.

RIVKA. *Some* may. Some may even beg you to do that rather than have the blood of a Christian on their hands. But others will say, no! Having bent the law for us, how often will they bend it for themselves and then we'll live in even greater uncertainties than before. They'll be divided, as you are, my clever brother. Who to save — your poor people or your poor friend? You can't see that?

SHYLOCK. We'll talk about it tomorrow.

RIVKA. It's not only your problem now, it's the community's. You can't see that?

SHYLOCK. Tomorrow, tomorrow.

RIVKA. And who *will* you choose? The one foreign friend you love or the families of your blood you barely know? (*Pause.*) Well, am I a fool or not? Are there to be jokes or not? Have you a problem or not?

SHYLOCK. Tomorrow, tomorrow. We'll talk about it tomorrow.

RIVKA. Tomorrow! Tomorrow! *What* tomorrow? The clocks will soon strike six and it will be tomorrow. (*Long pause. She rises to leave.*) Me you can get out of the way, your problem — not! (*She leaves.*)

SHYLOCK *turns to his letter.*

SHYLOCK (*aloud*). 'Reflect on our quarrels. They have said all. Your daughter, Jessica.' (*It is as though he has not understood.*) 'Our quarrels.' What quarrels? How could she have called them quarrels? *Enemies* quarrel. 'I am not what you would like me to be.' *What* did I want you to be, Jessica? My prop, my friend, my love, my pride? Not painful things, those. Are they?

Oh, Jessica. And where are you now? What wretched, alien philosophy has taken up your mind, muddied it with strange fervours? Which of the world's fervourists has lighted your sweet nature with its ephemeralties? Oh, vulnerable youth. You must be so lonely. So lost and lonely. So amazed and lost and lonely. Oh daughter, daughter, daughter.

ANTONIO *enters. He too appears burdened with worries. They confront each other in silent and all-knowing commiseration, then embrace.*

SHYLOCK *at once begins to fuss over his friend, sitting him down, pouring wine.*

SHYLOCK. It'll be all right. Your ships will find their harbour and my daughter will find her home.

ANTONIO. But whose harbour and whose home and when?

SHYLOCK. Ah! I see you're gloomy.

ANTONIO. And I see you pretend you're not.

SHYLOCK. And supposing you lose your ships, what? You've

no credit, no friends? What?

ANTONIO. I'm in debt to all Venice.

SHYLOCK. No skills to start again?

ANTONIO. Shylock, your own loss has stupefied you. Can you see me starting again? Wanting to? I've lived too long cushioned by huge sums, I'm not only naked without them, but my judgement's been flabbied by them.

SHYLOCK. Oh, now —

ANTONIO. Don't protest. You're evading the implications.

SHYLOCK. What, of a ship sinking or a daughter fleeing?

ANTONIO. Jessica's disappearance is a sad and awful thing, but other threats press.

SHYLOCK. Drink! I think we both need a little, little helpful drink.

ANTONIO. The implications must be faced and talked about.

SHYLOCK. Nothing presses, nothing threatens, drink.

ANTONIO. We've signed a foolish bond.

SHYLOCK. The bond will not be called upon — drink.

ANTONIO. It's known the ships were attacked, and my entire fortune staked in a single convoy. We've signed a foolish bond.

SHYLOCK. The storm will drop.

ANTONIO. We've signed a foolish bond, whose forfeiture is due.

SHYLOCK. The maritime office's fleet will sail — drink.

ANTONIO. At six o'clock there will be only twenty-four more hours to go.

SHYLOCK. Perhaps the days have been miscounted.

ANTONIO. SHYLOCK! (*Pause.*) What will you do with a knife in your hand and my flesh to weigh?

Long pause.

SOLOMON USQUE *and* REBECCA *arrive.*

REBECCA. Signor Shylock, is it true? We heard that your daughter is missing.

SHYLOCK. No commiserations, please. You're welcome. I love my friends around me, but there's been no death in my family, simply — a holiday. Every young person must have a holiday from home. Sit. I'll pour drink for you. Are you hungry? Tell me news.

REBECCA. Little change, families wanting passage to Constantinople, old men waiting for our funds for their voyage to Jerusalem, but your daughter, signor.

SHYLOCK. Who can write plays in such misery, eh, Signor Usque?

USQUE. No, who is there *great* enough to write plays in such misery!

SHYLOCK. Ah ha! Who is there great enough to write plays in such misery!

TUBAL *and a crestfallen* RODERIGUES *arrive.* SHYLOCK *looks to them expectantly.*

RODERIGUES. I told you! I warned! (TUBAL *stays him.*)

TUBAL. She has joined the man called Pisani.

SHYLOCK. Pisani?

TUBAL. They left tonight for an estate named Belmont.

SHYLOCK. Lorenzo Pisani? A nothing!

ANTONIO. To join Bassanio, my godson.

SHYLOCK. A man of whom it can only be said, 'He's there!' A sour, silly young man with little talent but that of envy, who confuses complaint for protestation, and even that betrays with a lazy mind. Jessica! you have been grabbed by air!

GRAZIANO *enters. Everyone knows what he has come to announce. They wait. He's terrified both of such an audience and the news he brings. He wants to hand the list to* ANTONIO.

ANTONIO. Read me the list. (*Pause.*) Yes, here.

GRAZIANO. A ship carrying raisins from the Island of Zante, olive oil from Corfu and the cotton from Syria. Another with wine, corn and cheese from Crete. The Danish ship you chartered for the English cloth and the Spanish wool. The assignment of timber and, the last, from —

ANTONIO. — from the sugar estates of Cyprus. All. They have taken or sunk the consignment I swore would be my last. I do not possess one ducat, Shylock.

A clock strikes six.

TUBAL *motions to the others that they should leave the two friends alone.*

ANTONIO. I cannot raise the money now.

SHYLOCK. I know.

ANTONIO. Nor can you lend it me again.

SHYLOCK. The Ghetto's drained, I know.

Long pause.

SHYLOCK. They'll let us drop the bond.

ANTONIO. We cannot, must not.

SHYLOCK. You understand?

ANTONIO. I understand.

SHYLOCK. I'm frightened that you don't.

ANTONIO. I do.

SHYLOCK. I will not bend the law.

ANTONIO. I understand.

SHYLOCK. I must not set a precedent.

ANTONIO. I know.

SHYLOCK. *You* said. *You* taught.

ANTONIO. Shylock, Shylock! I'm not afraid.

SHYLOCK. Oh friend! What have I done to you?

Pause.

ANTONIO. An act of schoolboy defiance when such times

should be taken seriously.

SHYLOCK. I know.

ANTONIO. Your yellow hat belongs to both of us. We shall both be put to death.

SHYLOCK. I know.

ANTONIO. I by you. You by them.

SHYLOCK. I know, I know.

ANTONIO. We know, we know! We keep saying we know so much.

SHYLOCK. Gently, gently, dear friend. I'm not afraid either.

Pause.

SHYLOCK. Just promise me silence in the trial.

ANTONIO. Will we make no explanations? The court must understand.

SHYLOCK. Understanding is beyond them! I protect my people and my people's contract. Besides, honour would be accorded me if I pleaded such explanations. 'He saved his people!' It would be grotesque. Just promise me silence at the trial.

ANTONIO. Silence, that's contempt, Shylock. Unworthy of you.

SHYLOCK. You must let my pride have its silence.

ANTONIO. They won't think it's pride, they will mistake your silence for contempt.

SHYLOCK. Perhaps they will be right. I am sometimes horrified by the passion of my contempt for men. Can I be so without pity for their stupidities, compassion for their frailties, excuses for their cruelties? It is as though these books of mine have spoken too much, too long; the massacres by kings, the deathly little spites of serfs, the oppressive jealousies and hurts of scholars, who had more learning than wisdom. Too much, Antonio, too much. Seeing what men have done, I know with great weariness the pattern of what

they will do, and I have such contempt, such contempt it
bewilders me. Surely, I say to myself, there is much to be
loved and cherished. I tell myself, force myself to remember.
Surely? Sometimes I succeed and then, ha! I'm a good man
to know, such a good man. Children warm to me in the
streets. They don't cry out 'Shylock Old Jew' then. No, they
skip at my side and hold my hand, and on those days I walk
so upright, like a young man, and I feel myself respected and
loved. And love I myself also. Why, you rush to ask, if such
joy comes to us through praising men, why do not we praise
them all the time? You ask! The balance, dear friend, the
balance! Take those books, one by one, place on one side
those which record men's terrible deeds, and on the other
their magnificence. Deed for deed! Healing beside slaughter,
building beside destruction, truth beside lie. (*Pause.*) My
contempt, sometimes, knows no bounds. And it has
destroyed me.

ANTONIO. Ah, Shylock, Shylock, why didn't we know one
another when young?

SHYLOCK (*smiling*). I'd have been wiser you mean?

ANTONIO. No, fool! It was myself I was thinking of.

SHYLOCK. I love thee, Antonio.

ANTONIO. And I thee, old man.

Scene Five

Belmont. The garden.

PORTIA. BASSANIO *enters with* LORENZO *and* JESSICA.

BASSANIO. My dear friends. What a pleasure to meet people
you love in new places. Lorenzo, here she is. You've heard
her described, now you see her in the flesh. Here, Portia, is
the man I spoke to you about — philosopher, prophet, a man
who may one day lead Venice — Lorenzo Pisani.

PORTIA. I hope, signor Lorenzo, you are not as intimidated by
what is expected of you as I feel stripped by the words
describing me! Nevertheless, says flesh to prophet: welcome!

BASSANIO. And Jessica welcome too. We've not met before
and so both Portia and I have this pleasure together.

PORTIA. Oh those sad eyes.

LORENZO. We're honoured and grateful for your hospitality
but those sad eyes carry sad news.

BASSANIO. Whose sad news?

LORENZO. Antonio's sad news. The ships are gone. The wreck
of one was found and it's assumed the others either shared
the same fate or have been taken off for use by the pirates.

PORTIA. But I don't understand the problem. Antonio owes
Shylock three thousand ducats. What's that? I'm able to raise
that sum and more besides to set him up in trade again.

LORENZO. No good! The hour is up and the Jew has turned
mad. He accepts no deviation from his contract and Antonio
insists upon sharing responsibility for it. The dilemma for the
Doge is unprecedented. 'My people! My bond! My people!
My bond!' as though the Jewish population were in threat
instead of a poor, beguiled friend of the Jew who must now
have the skin of his breast scraped from his bones.

JESSICA. Forgive me, Lorenzo . . . but . . .

LORENZO. You're right. My anger's made me indelicate.

JESSICA. It's not simply that —

BASSANIO. I warned him! A Jew to be trusted?

JESSICA. Please! Gentlemen! Remember me! I'm raw. My
rhythms still belong to the Ghetto. I can't slip so quickly
from God to God like a whore.

LORENZO. Jessica!

JESSICA. Yes, I'm also angry. You misrepresent the bond.
Whatever else my father's flaws you know the bond had
mockery not malice in it.

PORTIA. And that I understand. There's not enough of
mockery in Venice. We're a city boasting very little of
intelligent self-scrutiny or ridicule. But to mock the law is
one thing, to squeeze it of its last punitive drop is another.

JESSICA. He must have his reasons.

PORTIA (*warmly*). You must be hungry. Nerissa and I have prepared a light meal. Nothing too heavy.

BASSANIO. And I must go to prepare my luggage. Antonio will expect me to be near him while the court conducts its inquiries.

LORENZO. I'll join you, there's a principle affecting the future of Venice tied up in this case. Someone must air it.

BASSANIO (*leaving*). Forgive me?

PORTIA. The decision is yours. (*To* LORENZO.) I'll be very happy to look after your Jessica for you. It's a tragic affair but there's nothing we can do in it.

PORTIA *follows* BASSANIO *off*.

LORENZO. You look so sad. 'Those eyes'. They tell me I'm unworthy of you, that I don't appreciate your sacrifice. I do. Have courage. You've joined the world now.

JESSICA (*sardonically*). Is that what I've joined?

LORENZO. Come, lie in my arms these last minutes. You're shocked still. Let me tell you about yourself.

JESSICA (*trying to relax*). Oh do, Lorenzo, do tell me about myself, what I've done. Make sense of my actions for me. It seemed such a natural, inevitable thing to do. And now this bond, this wretched stupid bond threatens, threatens.

LORENZO. Hush, then.

JESSICA. I feel so full of discontent.

LORENZO. Quiet, then.

JESSICA. As though it's not in me ever to be happy.

LORENZO. Sssssssh!

JESSICA. I'm frightened and . . .

LORENZO. Sssssssh!

JESSICA. All right. I'm quiet. Look. Start.

LORENZO (*after a pause, portentously*). Some families are doomed.

JESSICA. That's not a very joyful start.

LORENZO. You should find all truths joyful.

JESSICA. Oh dear.

LORENZO. Even unhappy ones.

JESSICA. Oh dear, dear.

He wants to be solemn. She tries to be gay.

JESSICA. So, some families are doomed.

LORENZO. Parents have ill-chosen one another.

JESSICA. Parents have ill-chosen one another, so?

LORENZO. So, as parents can ill-choose one another, similarly can men ill-choose one another, similarly can men ill-choose their gods.

JESSICA, *slowly realising with disgust his meaning, rises angrily, and backs away.*

JESSICA. I see.

LORENZO. Not with those reproachful eyes, Jessica. You *know* that is the truth about yourself. The sadness Portia saw was also of a forsaken race, married to a God they'd thought had chosen them. Doomed!

JESSICA (*icily*). You think so?

LORENZO. But there are always survivors. I will make you a wife, a woman and a Christian.

JESSICA (*with controlled fury*). Sometimes I think the sadness in my eyes comes from the knowledge that we draw from men their desperate hates. Poisons rise in our presence, idiocies blossom, and angers, and incredible lapses of humanity. That is my doom! to know that secret: that at any time, for any reason, men are capable of such demented acts. So I regard a stranger, with dread, reproach, fear. Forever vigilant. That's difficult for him to bear, to be looked at like that, for no reason, to be thought guilty before the act, to be known for the beast in one, the devil in the making. Who can forgive eyes that have such knowledge in them?

LORENZO. I see there's a great deal of unthreading to do.

JESSICA. Yes, I see there is.

NERISSA *enters.*

NERISSA. Signor Lorenzo, you must leave at once. The wind is right. I've prepared food for your journey.

LORENZO. There's no better place to be left, Jessica.

He embraces her. She cannot respond.

Trust me, please.

LORENZO *leaves.*
JESSICA *looks very much alone.*
PORTIA *enters. At once, women together, they relax.*

PORTIA. Good, the three of us alone. Talk to me Jessica. Tell me about the Ghetto. My tutor in Hebrew studies was a strange man called Abraham Cardorso. *He* came from the Ghetto.

JESSICA. We knew him.

PORTIA. You did? What a coincidence.

JESSICA. Hardly a coincidence, madame, the quarter is so small.

PORTIA. And the buildings. So tightly packed together.

JESSICA. Yes. Always a danger of fire. Last week one young man, a friend in fact, threw himself into the flames attempting to save his mother. (*It's all too much for her. She is weeping. After a moment* —)

PORTIA. Tell me what you love in him.

JESSICA. I loved his questioning the wisdom of age, his clamouring to give youth its voice, his contempt for what men wrote in books. His strength, his seriousness, his devotion. I loved, I suppose, escape from oppressive expectations.

PORTIA. And now?

JESSICA. Now, I'm feeling his strength is arrogance, his seriousness is pedantry, his devotion is frenzy, and I am confused and drained and without ground beneath my feet.

PORTIA. And the truth about the bond?

JESSICA. Antonio asked my father for the loan which he would have given ten times over without a contract.

PORTIA. Shylock didn't want a contract?

JESSICA. Not with his dear friend, no. They almost quarrelled, till Antonio finally persuaded him — the law must be respected! The Jews have need of the laws of Venice and so — the bond, in defiance.

PORTIA. Then I understand nothing.

NERISSA. Why don't *you* attend the court in Venice, madame?

PORTIA. Attend the court in Venice?

NERISSA. Perhaps you'll understand more there.

PORTIA. And having understood, what then?

NERISSA. A word, a thought, have faith in that 'untried intellect'.

PORTIA. Faith in that 'untried intellect' I have, but knowledge of the law·I have none.

NERISSA. Perhaps it isn't law that's needed.

PORTIA. But there's so much work to do here.

NERISSA. Two men's lives are at stake.

PORTIA. But not men I know.

NERISSA. One, her father.

PORTIA. What can I do? I pity men their mad moments but a bond is a bond. The law demands its forfeitures. A pound of flesh is a satanic price to conceive, even as a joke but — (*She becomes a woman struck, as if by revelation. She can't believe the thought that has come to her. She rejects it but it persists.*) Holy Mary mother of Christ! I have it! But no. No! No, no, no, no, it's too simple. The law is complex, devious. This is common sense. Justice. The law is not to do with justice. No. It *can't* be applicable. And yet — who could possibly deny . . . the law may not be just when it demands strict adherence to an agreement which may cause misery,

but it does demand strict adherence. Then surely . . . dare I?
I'm no advocate. My temper's not for public places . . . and
yet . . . a wrong is a wrong . . .

JESSICA. To whom is she speaking?

PORTIA (*triumphantly*). Why don't we all three go to Venice
and attend the court? There is a contract I must scrutinise
and a father with whom you should be.

JESSICA. Are women granted entry to the courts?

PORTIA. They'll grant these women entry to the courts!

*The scene immediately becomes the courtroom of the
Doge's Palace.*

Scene Six

*The women turn and sweep into the courtroom of the Doge's
Palace, Venice.*
    PORTIA *and* NERISSA *walk straight up to ask the Doge
permission to enter. He grants it.* JESSICA *is embraced by*
RIVKA *and* TUBAL, NERISSA *moves to the Christian side.
Present are* USQUE, REBECCA, RODERIGUES *and*
SENATORS.
    (NOTE: *If the set can hide* PORTIA *from the proceedings,
good. If not, she must leave the court and reappear on her line.*)
    The YOUNG MEN *are surprised.*

BASSANIO. Portia!

LORENZO. Jessica!

BASSANIO. Did the women say they were coming?

LORENZO. On the contrary, Portia felt there was nothing to be
done.

BASSANIO. Nor is there. Silence! For two hours this court of
inquiry has had nothing but silence from him. Shylock! Will
you speak!

No response.

He says nothing, offers no explanation, simply claims the
bond.

JESSICA. Explain it to them, father, explain!

SHYLOCK *growls and turns away. He hates scorning her, but can't help himself. She retires in distress to the Christian side.*

BASSANIO. Look at that scowl. Have you ever seen such meanness in a face before? (*To* SHYLOCK.) He was your friend! You boasted a gentile for a friend!

GRAZIANO. When a man says nothing you can be sure he hides evil and guilt, you can be sure.

BASSANIO. But why hasn't Antonio said something?

GRAZIANO. Well, of course, he wouldn't. Bewitched wasn't he? Forced into the bond. (*Calling out.*) What did you say, old Jew? Not only would I be your friend, but I have to be your friend. Friendship? Ha!

BASSANIO. Shylock, will you speak!

LORENZO. Perhaps it's not Shylock who should speak but some of our own city councillors. Why were they silent? What Jewish money do they owe? It must be huge if they're prepared to let a fellow citizen be skinned alive. (*Calling out.*) Fellow Venetians, is this city so far gone in its quest for profit and trade that there's no morality left? Usury is a sin against charity. When God had finished his creation he said unto man and unto beasts, and unto fishes: increase and multiply, but did he ever say increase and multiply unto money?

ANTONIO. Profit is the fruit of skill, young man!

JESSICA. And this bond was the fruit of friendship, Lorenzo, not usury, you know it!

TUBAL. Besides, most people at some moments in their life become short of money — illness . . .

USQUE. . . . A bad harvest . . .

RODERIGUES. . . . Domestic misfortune . . .

TUBAL. What shall they do? I mean it's a problem!

LORENZO. I promise you that when the young patricians take their seats there'll be more God than Mammon on our statute books. Usury is a sin against charity. The —

TUBAL. And to deprive the people of an opportunity to obtain help is a sin against humanity!

LORENZO (*ignoring him*). Usury is a sin against charity. The —

TUBAL. Listen to me!

LORENZO. The people suffer from it!

ANTONIO. The people suffer from ignorance, Lorenzo, believe me. To deprive them of knowledge is the sin.

LORENZO. Knowledge! Knowledge! How Shylock's books have muddied your mind. A man can be strong and happy with no knowledge, no art. Turn to the shepherd and the tiller and the sailor who know of the evils of usury, without books, without art. Real knowledge, simple knowledge is in the wind and seasons and the labouring men do.

ANTONIO. You say a man is happy with no knowledge or art? There is wisdom in the wind, you say? The seasons tell all there is to know of living and dying? I wonder? Is it really understanding we see in the shepherd's eye? Is the tiller told more than the thinker? I used to think so, sitting with sailors roughened by salt, listening to their intelligence. They perceive much, I'd say to myself. But as I sat a day here, a day there, through the years, their intelligence wearied me. It repeated itself, spent itself upon the same complaints, but with no real curiosity. How alive is a man with muscles but no curiosity? You wonder why I bind my fate to Shylock, what I see in him? Curiosity! *There* is a driven man. Exhilarating! I thank the shepherd for my clothes and the tiller for my food, good men. Blessed. Let them be paid well and honoured. But they know, I, we know: there is a variousness to be had in life. Why else does the labourer send his sons to schools when he can? He knows what self-respect knowledge commands. All men do, wanting for their children what fate denied them, living without meat and keeping warm with mere sticks to do it. I'd have died before now if no man had kindled my soul with his music or wasn't there with his bright thoughts keeping me turning and taught about myself. Yes. Even at such an hour, I remember these things. Don't talk to me about the simple wisdom of the people, Lorenzo. Their simple wisdom is no more than the ignorance we choose to keep them in.

Silence.

GRAZIANO. As I thought. Bewitched. A knife hangs over him and he defends the man who holds it.

LORENZO. Be quiet, Graziano.

GRAZIANO. Lorenzo!

LORENZO. Stop meddling. You're a fool! The situation is too complex for you and I've not time for your tavern tattle.

BASSANIO. Quiet now. The Doge is ready.

The DOGE *returns to the official proceeding leaving* PORTIA *to continue perusing papers.*

DOGE. Antonio Querini?

ANTONIO (*stepping forward*). Most serene Prince.

DOGE. Shylock Kolner?

SHYLOCK. Most serene Prince.

DOGE. This court has never had before it such a case. The issue's clear, the resolution not. We must retrace and nag at it again. Signor Shylock, are you fully aware that the court is prepared to release both parties from the need to see this contract through?

SHYLOCK. I am, excellency.

DOGE. Yet you refuse, and state no reason?

SHYLOCK. I refuse and state no reason. Yes.

DOGE. And do you know this man may bleed to death?

SHYLOCK. I have our greatest doctors standing by.

DOGE. To do what? What can even Jewish doctors do to stem such awful draining of a man's life-blood? A strange perverted charity is that. You, Querini, dear fellow patrician, we beg you break your silence, or does this man have some hold over you? We've noticed your absence from the council's meetings. You once enjoyed the affairs of running our city, tell the court. Don't be afraid. What has happened?

ANTONIO (*impatiently*). Nothing has happened, excellency, more than I've lost my appetite for the intrigues and boredom of administration, but this has nothing to do with our humiliation in this court. Please, may we proceed.

DOGE. Then *you* say why we're here humiliated in this court. Say why you shared the madness of a bond which twice endangers you: from a man insisting that you pay a forfeiture of flesh, and from the law which must punish you for mocking it.

No response.

Your silence does not help.

GRAZIANO. I knew it! I told it! I warned it!

ANTONIO. Graziano, be quiet!

GRAZIANO. A plot! A plot! A Jewish plot!

ANTONIO. Be quiet, I say.

GRAZIANO. I can't be quiet, I love you.

ANTONIO. You love no one and nothing but a safe place with the multitude. Now be quiet.

DOGE. Why do you attack your friends, Antonio? These men who've come to speak for you? And why are you not speaking for yourself?

Pause.

LORENZO. Incredible! The man has even chained his victim to silence. Most serene Prince, I beg you —

DOGE. Be careful!

LORENZO. — the reason for humiliation in this court is linked with principles which go beyond this case.

DOGE. Do not attempt to make capital!

LORENZO. We should not be inquiring into silence but questioning if Jews and usury, no matter what the bond, should be permitted to pollute the fabric of our city's life. The real question is —

TUBAL. Do you think we enjoy the indignity of lending to your poor at twelve per cent . . .?

LORENZO. . . . the real question is . . .

RODERIGUES. Collect for your poor among yourselves!

LORENZO. . . . the real question is . . .

USQUE. You have pious fraternities, collect from them for your poor!

TUBAL. Or use taxes!

LORENZO. . . . THE REAL QUESTION IS . . .

DOGE. The question of the city's contracts with the Jews is a matter for the Council. The laws of Venice are very clear and precise and cannot be twisted this way and that for political significance or gain, nor denied to foreigners, otherwise justice will not obtain. And the principal foundation of our city, is justice. The people of Venice must have justice.

ANTONIO (*finally angry*). Justice? For the people of Venice? The people? When political power rests quite firmly in the hands of two hundred families? That, though he talks of principle, is what Lorenzo is impatient for, to share that power. You use the people's name, for through their grievances, you'll come to power. One of their grievances is what you call usury. The usurer's a Jew, and the Jew the people's favourite villain. Convenient! Easy! But the Jew pursues what he hates to pursue in order to relieve *us* of the sin. Usury *must* exist in our city, for we have many poor and our economy can't turn without it. Do we condemn the Jew for doing what our system has required him to do? Then if we do, let's swear, upon the cross, that among us we know of no Christian, no patrician, no duke, bishop or merchant who, in his secret chambers, does not lend at interest, for that is what usury is. Swear it! On the cross! No one, we know no one! (*Pause.*) Who's silent now? (*Pause.*) You will inflame the people's grievances in order to achieve power, Lorenzo, but once there you'll sing such different songs I think.

DOGE. You do not make inquiry easy for this court, Signor.

BASSANIO. How can you make inquiries into silence, most serene Prince, the inhuman silence of an arrogant chosen people. Heretical! They still refuse to acknowledge that they are no *longer* the chosen people.

SHYLOCK. Oh horror of horrors! Oh heresy of heresies! Oh sweat! Oh flutter! Oh butterflies, gooseflesh, hair-on-end! Oh windbag of windbags! And *you* I suppose, have been chosen instead?

LORENZO (*flooding the proceedings with conciliatory warmth and charm*). Most serene Prince. If my friend misapplies the word inhuman, we can perhaps understand. But I must pursue my original plea and ask the court to remember this: the Signor Shylock is not here because he is a Jew. The patricians of Venice are good men and justly fear being accused of such prejudice. No! What is on trial in this court is, I insist, the principle of usury whose evil this bond so tragically exemplifies, and from whose consideration we should not be detracted. The *bond* is inhuman, not the man. *No* one doubts the Jew is human. After all, has not a Jew eyes?

SHYLOCK. What is *that* fool attempting now?

LORENZO. Has not a Jew hands?

SHYLOCK. Is he presuming explanations on *my* behalf?

LORENZO. Has not a Jew organs, dimensions, senses, affections, passions?

SHYLOCK (*enraged*). Oh no!

LORENZO. Is not the Jew fed with the same food, hurt with the same weapons, subject to the same diseases, healed by the same means, warmed and cooled by the same winter and summer as a Christian is?

SHYLOCK. No, no!

LORENZO. If you prick him, does he not bleed?

SHYLOCK. No, no, NO! I will not have it. (*Outraged but controlled.*) I do not want apologies for my humanity. Plead for me no special pleas. I will not have my humanity mocked and apologised for. If I am unexceptionally like any man then I need no exceptional portraiture. I merit no special pleas, no special cautions, no special gratitudes. My humanity is my right, not your bestowed and gracious privilege.

GRAZIANO. See how ungrateful the Jew is? I knew it! I told it! I warned it! The Jew was silent because he knew that the moment he opened his mouth he'd hang himself with his arrogance. The Jew . . .

SHYLOCK (*furious but low and dangerous, building*) Jew! Jew, Jew, Jew! I hear the name around and everywhere. Your wars go wrong, the Jew must be the cause of it; your economic systems crumble there the Jew must be; your wives get sick of you — a Jew will be an easy target for your sour frustrations. Failed university, professional blunderings, self-loathing — the Jew, the Jew, the cause the Jew. And when will you cease? When, when, when will your hatreds dry up? There's nothing we can do is right. Admit it! You will have us all ways won't you? For our prophecies, our belief in universal morality, our scholarship, our command of trade, even our ability to survive. If we are silent we must be scheming, if we talk we are insolent. When we come we are strangers, when we go we are traitors. In tolerating persecution we are despised, but were we to take up arms we'd be the world's marauders, for sure. Nothing will please you. Well, damn you then! (*Drawing knife.*) I'll have my pound of flesh and not feel obliged to explain my whys and wherefores. Think what you will, you will think that in any case. I'll say it is my bond. The law is the law. You need no other reason, nor shall you get it — from me.

He turns to the DOGE, *justice must be done.* ANTONIO *joins him on the other side of the* DOGE. *They turn to face one another — doomed friends. Though no Jew must take another's life yet* SHYLOCK *has made the decision to damn his soul for the community which he feels is threatened.*

PORTIA. Most serene Prince, I have read the documents. (*Pause.*) Your Excellency, forgive my presumption, I know nothing of the law, but I cannot see that there is sufficient detail in this contract to make it legally valid.

Murmurs in court.

And if not valid, then not binding.

Excitement grows.

But I'm anxious in case my intelligence is merely foolish faith in little more than a hair of the law.

DOGE. The courts of Venice are open to justice no matter how tenuous a hair binds it to the law.

PORTIA. Then it seems to me this contract contains nothing but contradictions.

Tense silence.

There is in this bond a call for flesh but none for blood.

Noise in court.

There is in this bond a call for a precise pound weight but none for more or less.

Growing noise.

It cannot be executed because torn flesh draws blood.

Still growing noise.

It cannot be executed because precise weight cannot be achieved.

Yet more noise.

This contract is not binding because — impossible.

A swift silence in court.

SHYLOCK (*stunned, moves first to embrace* ANTONIO).
Thank God! Thank God! Of course! Idiots! Cut flesh draws blood. No blood no flesh. Oh, Antonio, how could such a simple fact escape us? Pedants of the law! Shame on you, a disgrace to your tribe. Go down Shylock, to the bottom of the class. Oh, Tubal, what a fool you've had for a partner. No wonder we never owned the really big warehouses. (*Offering knife to the three men.*) There! For you! *You* need it.

You've no wit to draw blood with your brains or tongue,
take this. Cruder, but guaranteed. Ha ha! No blood, no flesh.
I love the lady. Young lady I love you. You have a future, I
see it, a great future.

PORTIA (*with sadness*). But not you, old Shylock.

SHYLOCK. Not I? Are you mad? I've been delivered of murder
— I've got a clean and honest life to continue. Oh, not for a
hundred years, I know, and it's a pity because today,
TODAY I feel I want to go on living for ever and ever.
There's such wisdom in the world, such beauty in this life.
Ha! Not I, young lady? Oh yes, I! I, I, I! A great future, also.
Back to my books.

DOGE. No Shylock, no books.

SHYLOCK. No books? Will you take my books?

ANTONIO. You take his life when you take his books.

SHYLOCK. What nonsense now?

DOGE. No nonsense, I'm afraid, Shylock. An old Venetian law
condemns to death and confiscation of his goods the alien
who plots against the life of a citizen of Venice.

SHYLOCK. I? Plot? Against a citizen of Venice? Who?
Antonio?

DOGE. You pursued that which would end a man's life.

SHYLOCK. But was 'that' which I pursued 'plot'? Plot? Malice
aforethought?

DOGE. Malice aforethought or not, the end was a citizen's
death.

ANTONIO. However —

SHYLOCK. But there's no perception, no wisdom there.

ANTONIO. However —

SHYLOCK. As I warned, as I knew, no pity there.

GRAZIANO. Pity's called for now!

ANTONIO. HOWEVER! The law also says the offender's life is
at the mercy of the Doge —

DOGE. Which mercy I make no delay in offering you. But the State must take your goods. The people of Venice would not understand it if —

SHYLOCK. Oh! The people of Venice, of course.

LORENZO. See what contempt he has.

SHYLOCK. The people again. What strange things happen behind the poor people's name.

DOGE. — The people of Venice would not understand it if the law exacted no punishment at all for such a bond.

SHYLOCK. Of course.

ANTONIO. And I? What punishment do the people of Venice exact of me?

DOGE. Your foolishness, Signor, was punished by the pain of threatened death. Enough!

ANTONIO. The wisdom of patrician privilege, of course.

DOGE. But do not strain it, friend. Do not.

ANTONIO (*bowing*). I thank you.

The DOGE *and all leave, except* SHYLOCK, ANTONIO, PORTIA, JESSICA.

SHYLOCK (*turning to* PORTIA). And the lady, where is the lovely lady, what does she say to all this?

PORTIA (*with sad apology*). The lovely lady can say nothing more to merit the name.

SHYLOCK (*tenderly, as to a daughter*). All that intelligence? Gone?

PORTIA. Not gone, but limited in power. Your lovely lady used her common sense to read a bond. That is the best not only she could do, but can be done. The law takes over now.

SHYLOCK (*sardonically*). Oh! I forgot! The law. Yes. Impartial justice. Is that to be applied now?

PORTIA (*poignantly*). Oh, Signor Shylock, please don't look to me for help.

SHYLOCK. There, there! I'm sorry. Shuh, shuh.

PORTIA (*raging at the departed* DOGE). I would not carry a sword in one hand and scales in the other. That image always seemed to me ambiguous. Is my sword held high to defend the justice my left hand weighs? Or is it poised threateningly to enforce my left hand's obduracy?

SHYLOCK. Impartial justice, lovely lady, impartial justice.

PORTIA. Impartial? How? *I* am not a thing of the wind, but an intelligence informed by other men informed by other men informed! *I* grow. Why can't they? What *I* thought yesterday might be wrong today. What should I do? Stand by my yesterdays because *I* have made them? I made today as well! And tomorrow, that I'll make too, and all my days, as my intelligence demands. I was born in a city built upon the Wisdom of Solon, Numa Pompilius, Moses!

They exchange sad smiles.

SHYLOCK (*shrugs*). What can one do?

PORTIA. Wisdom, inconsiderately, does not translate in a moment.

They exchange another smile.

SHYLOCK (*with sad pleasure, taking her hand, still as to a daughter*). You have a future, young lady, I tell you, a great future.

JESSICA *finds this tender moment between her father and another young woman unbearable and flees.*

ANTONIO. Shylock! Don't be a stubborn old man. Explain to the court you did not want to set a precedent in law. You'll save your books.

SHYLOCK (*sardonically and with finality*). No. Take my books. The law must be observed. We have need of the law, what need do we have of books? Distressing, disturbing things, besides. Why, dear friend, they'd even make us question laws. Ha! And who in his right mind would want to do that? Certainly not old Shylock. Take my books. Take everything. I do not want the law departed from, not one letter departed from.

Sound of song.

Perhaps now is the time to make that journey to Jerusalem. Join those other old men on the quayside, waiting to make a pilgrimage, to be buried there — ach! What do I care! My heart will not follow me, wherever it is. My appetites are dying, dear friend, for anything in this world. I am so tired of men.

SHYLOCK *moves away, a bitter man. Everyone has left except* PORTIA. *The scene has changed to Belmont. We hear the distant sad singing of a woman. The song is 'Adio querida', a Sephardic song.**

Scene Seven

Belmont. The garden. A warm, heavy, melancholy evening. PORTIA *strolling,* JESSICA *stands aside.*
    The woman singing in the distance.
    The air is broken by the sound of raucous laughter.
BASSANIO, LORENZO *and* GRAZIANO *enter carrying food.* NERISSA *follows them. A picnic is prepared.*
    They talk, spread a rug, light candles while NERISSA *prepares platters of food.*

BASSANIO. A farewell supper! Our friends are leaving, Portia. Tonight must be made memorable. Lorenzo! Jessica! Food!

But they seem reluctant to join the three young men. LORENZO *alone notes the indifference, especially of* JESSICA.

GRAZIANO. It's a splendid house. The most beautiful I've seen. Really, Signorina Contarini, splendid. About two hundred and twenty-three years old, I'd say. And what a library! It made me pick up a book for the first time in years.

LORENZO (*acidly*). Which book?

GRAZIANO. No, no, Lorenzo. You can't keep getting at me. We've been through a lot together now and you know me to be your faithful admirer. I know my limitations and I'm

*See EMI label ASD 2649, sung by Victoria de los Angeles.

happy to be factotum to your cause. Or causes. Name them,
I'll follow. Plot them, I'll execute them. Don't be ungracious.
There's a lot to be said for a sycophant.

ANTONIO *appears.*

PORTIA. I'm so grateful you stayed, Signor Querini. These two
weeks have been made bearable, and I've found a new friend.

ANTONIO. While I've found a woman who's made me mourn
my youth. What mixed blessings in these last years of my
life, to meet an acerbic old Jew who disturbed my dull
complacency; and you, blossoming with purpose, reminding
me of a barren life. An unfair restlessness at this depleted
age. (*Pause.*) He will haunt me, that man.

Silence but for the singing.

What will you do?

PORTIA. Honour my father's wishes, marry the man who chose
lead, dutifully take my role of wife, look to what must be
grown. And you?

ANTONIO. Sort out what has been salvaged from my ships. See
my friend off to the holy land. Visit him, once, perhaps,
before I die, and you often, if I may, before I die.

PORTIA. Oh please! I would be so indebted.

ANTONIO. But what will happen to her?

LORENZO (*calling her to eat*). Jessica!

*She ignores him. He waits throughout the next exchange for
her to turn to him. She does turn, contemptuously, then
turns away.*

PORTIA. I'll look after Jessica. My marriage is a parent's will,
not hers, though. Mine can't be held back, hers, I will see,
never takes place.

ANTONIO. But *which* place will she take? There's no father's
house to return to.

PORTIA. But there is a Jerusalem, where he can be followed.

ANTONIO. I don't think I really fear for Jessica, but you . . .

PORTIA. I! I'll fill my house with poets and philosophers, and politicians who are poets and philosophers. Bassanio will come to know his place, accept it, or leave it. I am to be reckoned with, you know, not merely dutiful. Although, something in me has died struggling to grow up.

LORENZO *turns angrily away from looking at* JESSICA, *finally understanding that he's lost her.*

LORENZO. I don't think I shall ever lose the image of that man's scowl from my mind. Remember? And how silent he was, to begin with.

GRAZIANO. To begin with he would be, very silent.

LORENZO. Fortunately the law is a terrifying thing and the courts are an awesome place.

GRAZIANO. Ha! But he was awed.

BASSANIO. 'And you I suppose have been chosen instead!' How he spat the words out. A man full of despite and contempt.

PORTIA *and* ANTONIO *move away to different corners of the garden. They, with* JESSICA, *are three lonely points of a triangle which now encircle the grating sounds of an inane conversation.*

LORENZO. Perhaps now they will learn, the elders. Virtue consists in simplicity, suffering, renunciation!

GRAZIANO. But we forget Portia, his wife . . .

BASSANIO. Not yet, not yet!

GRAZIANO. His wife to *be*. Now there's a mind to be careful of. Should we envy him or fear for him?

BASSANIO. It was in my stars to make such a match for my bed.

GRAZIANO. You're mad to think only of bed with an intellect like that at your side.

BASSANIO. It shall be cherished but not spoilt. I shall turn to it but not let it rule! Ah! Here comes Nerissa with drink for the heroes.

NERISSA. And heroes you are, sirs, true. No denying it. True, true, heroes indeed. True. True, true, true. Heroes!

Only the singing now and a fading, warm and sad evening.

Notes

Act 1

1   *Ghetto Nuovo* — 'ghetto' in Venetian dialect meant 'iron foundry', and the Venetian Jews had to live on the site of a former ironworks in Venice. From this, 'ghetto' has become the term for any segregated district enclosing a minority group away from the rest of the population.

1   *loan-banker* — money lender.

1   *Maimonides* — Jewish philosopher (1135—1204), evolved an important philosophy of religion, of which the *Guide to the Perplexed* is the classic work.

1   *R. David Kimhi* — Jewish grammarian (1160—1235); his grammar and lexicon are the basis of most similar subsequent work.

2   *Talmudic Law* — the Talmud is the major post-biblical Jewish writing, consisting of a commentary on Hebrew law assembled from learned discussions between rabbis.

2   *Campo dei Fiore* — open space or square in Rome; in mediaeval times often a place of execution.

2   *Julius the Third* — (1487—1555) elected pope 1550. Known for nepotism and licentious living.

2   *Council of Ten* — an executive body in the Venetian government, parallel to the Senate, which dealt with affairs of public safety and morals, and also with foreign affairs, where its jurisdiction could overrule the Senate.

2   *the Sacred Books* — i.e. the Talmud.

3   *Bomberg* — David Bomberg, active in Venice 1516—1549, a famous Christian printer of Hebrew books, produced the first complete printed edition of the Talmud in 1520—3.

3   *Isaac of Corbeil* — died 1280; a French codifier, wrote a very popular work on the law.

3   *additamenta* — added material, such as notes written in the margins.

3   *Daniel* — a prophet in the Old Testament.

3   *Messianic times* — the time of the coming of the Messiah or Saviour; the Messiah is identified by Christians as Jesus Christ, but

by some Jews with the modern state of Israel, while others believe
the Messiah is yet to come.

3   *gondola* — characteristic and graceful boat used by the
Venetians for moving along the canals that are the 'streets' of
Venice.

3   *Sabbath* — the day of rest, Saturday for Jews, Sunday for
Christians, on which the Bible forbids any work to be done.

3   *Crete . . . Corfu* — islands in the Mediterranean sea,
convenient for trade with Venice.

4   *ducats* — coins of the Venetian currency.

4   *Martyrs of Blois* — Blois in France was the scene of the first
ritual murder charge against Jews in Europe in 1171, after which
thirty-one Jewish men and women were burnt at the stake.

4   *Rabbi Yom Tov of Joigny* — a Jewish Liturgical poet, died
1190.

5   *massacre of London* — there was a murderous attack on the
London Jews at the time of the coronation of Richard I in 1189.

5   *massacre of York* — the York Jews were besieged in the
Castle Keep and killed each other rather than surrender (1190).

5   *semites* — persons whose native tongue belongs to the semitic
group of languages, including Arabs, Israelis, Ethiopians,
Babylonians, Canaanites.

5   *Abraham* — the patriarch in the Old Testament, and an
important figure in Jewish, Christian and Moslem faiths.

6   *godson* — when a child is baptised, promises are made on his
behalf by godfathers and godmothers; it was expected that
godparents would use influence, if any, on behalf of their
godchildren.

6   *patrician* — a member of the large caste whose ancestors had
sat on the great council of Venice from 1171 to 1380. Their
ancestry and relationships were carefully recorded, and they alone
had the right to vote for the members of the senate.

6   *not the type* — as an 'ungodly' bachelor, Antonio is not
suited to the religious responsibilities of a godfather.

6   *just the type* — as a rich bachelor with no other
responsibilities, Antonio is available as a benefactor to his godson
in material affairs.

6   *in ten minutes* — a curfew forbade Jews to be outside the
boundaries of the Ghetto after a certain hour of the evening, and
also forbade gentiles to remain inside after that hour.

7   *Abtalion da Modena* — (1529—1611) distinguished as a
scholar: his impressive and learned plea to Pope Gregory XIII in

1581 reprieved Jewish books from the threat of burning.

7   *Solomon Usque* — (1530—95) translated Petrarch into
Spanish, wrote a play and poetry; settled at the end of his life in
Constantinople.

7   *Rabbi* — literally 'teacher', master; honorary title given to
scribes and ordained scholars.

7   *synagogue* — Jewish house of worship.

7   *Aristotle* — Greek philosopher (384—322 BC).

10   *Anusim* — literally, 'constrained', also called 'Maranos'; these
Spanish and Portuguese Jews pretended to be Christian to avoid
persecution but also followed their Jewish religion in secrecy.

10   *Inquisition* — a tribunal established by the Papacy in Spain,
Italy and Germany to detect and punish heresy. The Spanish
Inquisition was reorganised in 1478 to make it more effective
against the Jews who were alleged to be plotting against the
government; and it became dependent upon the Spanish monarchy.

12   *citronade* — drink made from citrons, a fruit like a lemon.

12   *match-making* — planning marriages.

12   *Coimbra Tribunal* — tribunal of a town in Beira province,
Portugal.

12   *autos-da-fé* — literally 'acts of faith', at which the sentences
of the Inquisition on its victims were read. Those convicted were
handed over to the state for torture or execution.

12   *Traz-os-Montes and Beira* — provinces of Portugal.

12   *Evora* — district of Portugal.

12   *Braganza* — administrative district and city in Traz-Os-Montes,
Portugal.

12   *Guarda* — Portuguese city in Beira.

12   *Lamego* — Portuguese town in Beira.

13   *Ancona* — town on the Adriatic coast, the only good port
between Venice and Brindisi.

13   *Salonika* — coastal town on the gulf of Salonika.

14   *Constantinople* — modern name: Istanbul; former capital of
the eastern part of the Roman Empire, later capital of Turkey after
its capture by the Turks. Venice was involved in its affairs.

14   *The Fox's Fables* — one of the most widely popular of
English books.

14   *Exeter Cathedral* — a cathedral in England; its library
contained rare manuscripts and other works.

15   *German Synagogue* — there were originally five synagogues in
the Ghetto.

17   *Palladio* — Andrea Palladio (1518—80), Italian architect, at

one time chief architect of Venice, renowned for his own 'Palladian'
style which revived classical Roman features.

17   *San Giorgio Maggiore* — one of the most famous churches in
Venice, designed by Palladio.

17   *plan-blind* — i.e. unable to see the meaning of plans.

20   *Rialto* — area of Venice near the Rialto bridge, meeting place
of Venetian businessmen.

21   *no pork* — the Jewish religion forbids eating pork.

22   *Moses of Castelazzo* — a portrait painter, known throughout
Italy during the fifteenth and sixteenth centuries.

24   *collateral* — an additional security, as well as the prospective
profits of the voyages themselves.

24   *Deuteronic Code* — i.e. in the book of Deuteronomy in the
Bible.

26   *spice pebbles* — many spices take the form of seeds looking
like pebbles before they are ground.

27   *dead thing* — this was the traditional objection to lending
money at interest.

27   *Virgin Marys* — biblical subjects were very popular with
painters.

29   *Savonarola* — (1452–98) a Domenican monk, an Italian, who
preached against the corruptions of his time, denouncing not only
materialism but also worldly literature. His extremism led to
reaction and he was executed.

30   *Doge* — head of the Venetian state.

30   *Orso* — a doge of Venice.

30   *Anafesto* — the first doge of Venice, elected 697.

30   *Roman Empire* — it is the legal and social achievements of
the Roman Empire, not its military skill, that Venice particularly
aspired to.

33   *Catherine of Aragon* — first wife of Henry VIII of England,
though earlier married to his elder brother, Arthur, who died
young. The pope gave a dispensation for her to marry her late
husband's brother, which was normally not permitted.

33   *Charles V* — Emperor of Germany. He was Catherine of
Aragon's nephew and annulment of her marriage would offend him.

33   *Leviticus* — i.e. 18, verse 16.

33   *Deuteronomy* — i.e. 24, verse 5.

38   *yellow hat* — the Jews had to wear yellow (later, red) hats to
distinguish them from the other Venetians.

39   *Tintoretto* — (1518–94) the last great master of the Venetian
school of painters.

39   *Ezekiel* — Hebrew prophet of the 6th century BC, whose oracles are contained in the biblical book that bears his name.

39   *Jeremiah* — a prophet from Judah (c. 626—587 BC), whose oracles are also contained in the biblical book that bears his name.

41   *Roman Wars* — there were various rebellions against the Roman rule of Judea in the first century AD. That of 66 AD was followed by Roman military dominance and enslavement of large numbers of Jews.

41   *Cassiodorus* — statesman and man of learning, born c 480 AD, who collected a library and composed many works after his retirement to the monastery at Bruttium.

42   *Bruttii* — Cassiodorus founded the monastery of Viviers in Bruttium, the extreme southern part of Italy.

42   *Benedictines* — the order of monks who profess to follow the rules of St Benedict.

42   *German Holy Roman Empire* — the German Emperor, Charles the Great (Charlemagne), with the consent of the pope, took power over the western part of the former Roman Empire, the eastern part being ruled from Constantinople.

42   *Anjou* — this French dynasty is associated with the history of Naples.

43   *Aragon* — area of Spain; at one time a separate kingdom.

43   *City States* — Italy was for a long time fragmented into small territories around its cities which each had its separate government.

44   *Mayence* — Mainz, in Germany.

44   *Gutenberg* — German printer (1397—1468); invented, or possibly developed from unknown experimenters, the method of printing by moveable type.

44   *Manutius* — Manutius Aldus (1449—1515), typographer and scholar.

44   *Aldine editions* — so called after Manutius Aldus, who printed them.

Act 2

45   *Beirut* — seaport on the Mediterranean coast, in Syria.

45   *Famagusta* — seaport on the coast of Cyprus.

45   *Dalmatian towns* — Dalmatia was the narrow coastal area on the east side of the Adriatic.

45   *Treviso and Vicenza* — north Italian towns close to Venice and at some periods subject to her.

46   *commit you in marriage* — it was common for families to arrange marriages for their children when young; they might be betrothed or even married at a very early age.

47   *Hebrew* — the language spoken by the Israelites during most of the time of their national existence in Palestine, and in which nearly all their sacred works were written; later forms of the language were used for literary purposes by Jewish writers throughout the middle ages and to the present day.

48   *Church* — the Roman Catholic Church.

48   *Plato and Aristotle* — classical Greek writers of the fourth century BC.

48   *Ovid and Catullus* — classical Roman poets of the first century BC.

48   *a woman on the English throne* — Queen Elizabeth the First of England.

48   *capital* — supply or amount of money.

49   *Seneca* — classical Roman dramatist of the first century BC.

51   *minutiae* — small details.

52   *gimcrack* — of inferior materials.

62   *Zante* — island off the east coast of Greece.

63   *serfs* — workers on the land, legally bound to the land on which they live.

71   *Mammon* — pagan god representing love of money.

73   *tavern tattle* — gossip.

73   *Most serene* — the correct way to address the doge.

74   *to make capital* — to exploit something to one's own advantage.

81   *Solon* — c. fifth century BC, a Greek statesman, who reformed the constitution of Athens.

81   *Numa Pompilius* — the second king of ancient Rome, famous for his wisdom and piety and as a giver of laws.

81   *Moses* — Old Testament prophet, lawgiver to his people, to whom he brought down God's commandments from Mount Sinai.

82   *Adio querida* — goodbye my darling.

82   *Sephardic* — Spanish and Portuguese Jews as opposed to the Ashkenazy Polish and German Jews.

84   *in my stars* — predestined, as shown by the configurations of the stars.

John Dexter directing the New York production (Photo:
Richard Braaten)

The New York production. *Left*: Shylock. *Above*: the portrait scene. *Below*: Shylock and Rivka. (Photos: Martha Swope)

The New York production. *Left*: Portia and Bassanio. *Above*:
Lorenzo and Jessica. *Below*: Shylock and Antonio. (Photos:
Martha Swope)

Nerissa and Portia in the New York production. (Photo: Martha Swope)

The last scene in Belmont: Antonio, Nerissa and Lorenzo (at back), Graziano and Bassanio (in front). New York production. (Photo: Martha Swope)

The Danish premiere at Arhus. *Left*: Shylock, Rivka and Portia. *Above*: Antonio and Shylock. *Below*: the trial scene. (Photos: Rolf Linder)

DATE DUE			

Wesker   209325